A LIFE UNNOTICED

SUSANNAH COULTAS
AND HER FAMILY IN VICTORIAN SUFFOLK

By

Anne Coultas Dunford

To Muriel
with very best wishes
from Anne

Published 2005 by arima publishing

www.arimapublishing.com

ISBN 1-84549-044-4

Printed and bound in the United Kingdom

Typeset in Garamond 11.5/16

arima publishing
ASK House, Northgate Avenue
Bury St Edmunds, Suffolk IP32 6BB
t: (+44) 01284 700321

www.arimapublishing.com

Cover Photographs:
- Houses in The Street Parham, 2004. The Coultas family lived in this street.
- Farnham Church, 2004. Susannah Coultas was christened here.
- Snape Bridge, 2004. Susannah Coultas loved to visit this spot in the 1860s and 1870s.
- Framlingham Castle, 2005.
- Susannah Coultas, 1891.

*For Sarah and Chris
and in memory of Andrew*

*Fallentis semita vitae
The pathway of a life unnoticed
Horace 68–65 B C
Epistles bk. 1 no. 18, 1. 103*

About the Author

Anne Coultas Dunford was born near Guildford, Surrey and moved to Suffolk in 1962 where she still lives. She qualified as a solicitor and has spent a lifetime in voluntary youth work. She was appointed OBE in 1998 for services to Guiding.

Contents

Chapter One

Introduction – Journey to Suffolk

My first visit to Suffolk was in August 1949. I was fourteen and had come with my parents, Arthur and Meg Tunnell, for our summer holiday in Felixstowe. It was a surprise when I heard where we were going; living near Guildford in Surrey as we did, we usually holidayed in the south or west of England. All through the Second World War we enjoyed holidays in Devon, and other seaside holidays took us to places such as Eastbourne or the Isle of Wight. I knew nothing of Suffolk, and was puzzled that my mother was so keen to explore this seemingly far distant county north of the River Thames.

The journey was quite an adventure in itself. My father's eyesight was not good enough to drive, and it would never have occurred to my mother to take driving lessons. This meant we had to take a bus to the station, a Southern Railway train to London Waterloo and then the Underground, a steam train to Ipswich, and finally a branch line train to Felixstowe. It seemed an endless day of travelling, particularly as the trains were crowded and sometimes we had to throw our suitcases into the carriage through the window in order to reserve a seat! I well remember carrying my heavy brown case (no wheeled luggage in those days) across the road from Felixstowe Station to catch a bus outside what is now the Elizabeth Orwell Hotel. My parents, born in 1890 and 1894 and therefore in their fifties, were understandably tired after such a long and disjointed journey, but we all brightened up when the bus took us down the hill to the sea front and we arrived at last at our hotel. Luckily the beach was close by, so it was easy to walk there, enjoy the sunshine and meet new young friends beside the sea.

As the holiday progressed I discovered why we had come. Meg's mother Susannah, whose maiden name was Coultas, had apparently been born in Suffolk, and she wanted to see some of the places that Susannah had remembered from her youth. We journeyed (it must have been in a chauffeur-driven car) to Farnham and Saxmundham, to Snape Bridge across the River Alde and Snape Maltings and finally to Framlingham. The day passed in something of a blur – as a teenager I had little interest in family history and did not understand the significance of my mother's searching. I enjoyed the holiday but forgot about most of it once I had returned to Surrey and school.

Years later however, in 1961, an estate agent's advertisement in a national newspaper caught my eye. It was for houses for sale in Suffolk, at a time when my new husband and I were keen to move out of the London area and settle in the country. We came to look at the properties being advertised, and although we found it almost impossible to understand the Suffolk dialect and didn't much like the houses when we saw them, we did fall in love with the area and managed to find both work and a new home in Ipswich.

My travels have taken me to many places in this beautiful East Anglian county over the years, but it is only recently that I have begun to trace my family's roots in Suffolk. In retrospect, it was fitting that my first journey to Felixstowe took me by train, since I now know that my great grandfather and his brother-in-law played a small part in building and running the county's rail system in the mid-nineteenth century. The more I researched, the more I unearthed a fascinating story: a story of one ordinary family in Suffolk in Victorian times, whose lives came to be influenced, in difficult circumstances, through the actions of two rather extraordinary men.

Chapter Two

Family Origins

North Grimston Church, East Riding of Yorkshire, where Robert Coultas and Ann Marshall were married in 1811.

The family of Susannah Coultas can be traced back to Yorkshire. Her grandfather Robert Coultas was baptised at Wykeham near Scarborough on October 6th 1786 and married Ann Marshall in 1811 at the parish church of North Grimston in the East Riding. (1) There were many Coultas families in this part of Yorkshire in the eighteenth and nineteenth centuries, although it is a less usual surname nowadays. Some sources suggest that it originated in the Lanarkshire area of Scotland, while P H Reaney, in his *'Dictionary of British Surnames'*, lists a William Cowthus in 1562 and John Coultas, Coultus, Cowtus in 1657, 1671, 1691 and 1733, all recorded in the Register of the Freemen of York. The earliest record of the name in the International Genealogical Index shows the marriage of a Thomas Coltas to Margaret Holdsworth in Halifax, Yorkshire in 1559. The name is said to mean 'worker at the colt-house, colt-keeper'. Reaney also makes reference to a John le Coltere in 1327 in the Suffolk Subsidy Rolls – a derivative of the Old English 'colt' – A keeper of colts'. (2)

Robert Coultas was described as a husbandman [a farmer; a man who tills and cultivates the soil] whose farm was at North Grimston. Sometimes called Grimstone, it was a small agricultural village about four miles south east of Malton. The parish church, dedicated to Saint Nicholas, is of grey stone, with an impressive Norman dog-tooth arch leading to the chancel, where Robert and Ann would have been married. Their first seven children were all christened at North Grimston, presumably in the large stone font (possibly large enough for immersion) that dates from Saxon times and has wonderful carvings of Saint Nicholas, The Last Supper and The Crucifixion.

Around 1824, Robert and his wife Ann began a new life at Greasley in Nottinghamshire, from where he seems to have farmed extensively in Watnall, Beauvale and Arnold. Their remaining seven children were all christened at Greasley Church between 1825 and 1837. Ann Coultas, the tenth child of Robert and Ann, was christened at Greasley on May 4th 1829 while her brother James, their twelfth child, was christened there on March 9th 1833. Ann Coultas married Isaac Allcock in 1849 at Greasley and by 1863 they had seven children. Their eldest son, Robert Allcock, was born in 1849 in Nottinghamshire, but Ann and Isaac must have moved around with his work as their next son Isaac was born in 1851 in Riddings ('Ridings' on the Census records) in Derbyshire, a third son George was born in 1852 and then a daughter Ann/e was born in 1854 in Hereford. By 1858 the family had moved to East Suffolk to settle in the village of Benhall, not far from Saxmundham. Their three remaining children were born there: Alice in 1858, John George in 1861 and Charles Marshall Allcock in 1863. Sadly third son George did not survive for long after they arrived in Suffolk. He was to die in 1859 aged just six and a half. (3)

Isaac Allcock was described in some records as a railway labourer and in others as a Great Eastern railway servant, but on the 1861 and 1871 censuses his occupation was railway inspector. No doubt therefore it was because of his work with the railways that he travelled outside Nottinghamshire and then came to Suffolk, to work on parts of the Great Eastern Railway under construction or newly laid at that time. In 1871 the family were living at Railway Cottage in Benhall, and it is possible that Isaac's promotion to inspector came with his move to Suffolk. It was probably a supervisory, middle management job, but what he inspected is not recorded: it could have been the track, signals or engines, goods, carriages or railway staff, or perhaps the station itself or the passengers' tickets.

Chancel Arch and Saxon Font, North Grimston Church. The first seven children of Robert and Ann Coultas were christened here.

After growing up in Nottinghamshire, Ann and Isaac must have taken a while to adapt to Suffolk and its way of life, not least to its dialect and customs. Certainly Agnes Strickland, who lived between 1796 and 1879, found the people of Suffolk somewhat different from the norm:

They are in sooth, a peculiar people, in respect, not only to their dialect and idioms, but to their modes of thinking and acting. Their racy peculiarities and their Saxon phraseology are, however, fast disappearing before the innovation of the so-called civilization, which the introduction of railroads and the progress of luxury are making in the primitive habits of this "angle of the isle". Suffolk men are so opposed to anything allied to change that it will take more than a century to render the portraitures of the present generation obsolete'. (4)

Reluctance to change appears even now to be a Suffolk characteristic; when I arrived in the county I was told that it would take forty years before I was accepted (though in fact I received warm welcomes from the start) and then someone told me that was quite wrong: it should have been fifty, not forty years!

It was also a county where a variety of superstitions persisted in Victorian times. Writing in his *'New Suffolk Garland'* in 1866, John Glyde described several omens of good or ill luck:

'...amongst Suffolk people to sneeze three times before breakfast is a pledge that you will soon have a present made to you. The sneezing of a cat however is considered to be an evil omen; it is a sign that the family of the owner will all have colds.

It is usual in this county to communicate family secrets to the bees, such for instance as a birth or death. If neglected on such occasions, the bees are apt, it is said, to take offence, and to move to other residences where they will be treated with more confidence. They are said to be so sensitive as to leave houses, the inmates of which indulge in swearing.

If you break two things, you will break a third. A lady saw one of her servants take up a coarse earthenware basin, and deliberately throw it down on the brick floor. "What did you do that for?" asked the mistress. "Because, ma'am, I'd broke tew things," answered the servant; "so I thout the third 'd better be this here", pointing to the remains of the least valuable piece of pottery in the establishment, which had been sacrificed to glut the vengeance of the offended ceramic deities.' (5)

Suffolk in the mid-nineteenth century was predominantly an agricultural county, but one affected by the changes and challenges of an industrial age. David Dymond and Peter Northeast, in *'A History of Suffolk'*, state that

'A growing population and rising unemployment were the basic cause of many problems in the 19th century. Suffolk's population increased by over 50 per cent in the first half of the century, passing 335,000 in 1851 and 380,000 by 1901. This increase was despite the large numbers of people leaving the county to settle in other parts of Britain or abroad.' (6) *'For the only time in English history, the 1851 Census showed equal numbers of people living in towns and villages. Thereafter, towns continued to grow at the expense of the countryside.'* (7)

In *'The Royal Illustrated History of the Eastern Counties'* A D Bayne gave the following account of Suffolk's agriculture and industry in 1873:

The productions of the county are wheat, barley, peas, beans, seeds of various kinds, mangolds, turnips and other roots. The wheat is of excellent quality, and usually commands a high price. The barley is amongst the best grown in England, and is largely malted for the Burton and other large breweries. Mangel wurtzel and turnips are grown of great weight and good quality for grazing purposes. Some farmers grow flax in the neighbourhood of Eye, Debenham, and Framlingham; and factories are in operation for preparing the flax. There is a great whole-sale trade in cattle, corn, malt, etc., at different markets in the county, especially Ipswich and Bury. Suffolk manufacturers are such as are in some way connected with agriculture.

There is no other part of England containing so many manufacturers of engines and machines for agricultural purposes, or where the implements of husbandry are made more perfect than in Suffolk...' (8)

Leading innovators and manufacturers of agricultural machinery included firms such as Ransome of Ipswich, Garrett of Leiston, Smyth of Peasenhall and Boby of Bury (St Edmunds). (9)

Back in Nottinghamshire, Ann's brother James Coultas (my great grandfather) was working as a greengrocer in Trowell near Nottingham when he married Eliza Hallam on January 23rd 1859 at Beeston Parish Church. James' parents had died by this time (his mother Ann in 1838 and his father Robert in 1854) and Eliza's father was also dead before the wedding took place, so the witnesses were James' elder sister Susannah and her husband Thomas Clifford. James was able to write his name, but Eliza could not. Like so many other people at that time, in the days before education was compulsory, she signed the marriage register with a cross as her mark.

Chapter Three

Work on the Railways

Framlingham Castle, 1904, with ivy and trees obscuring the walls as they did when James and Eliza Coultas lived in the town.

Within months of their marriage, James had given up his greengrocer's job and he and Eliza had travelled east to join Ann and Isaac Allcock in Suffolk. It seems likely that Ann and Isaac had told James there was good work to be had on the county's railways and encouraged him to make the move. Working for a railway company could bring better wages and prospects. As Trevor May states in 'The Victorian Railway Worker',

'*often agricultural workers (were) attracted by higher rates of pay (on the railways). In Northamptonshire for example in the mid 1830s, a farm labourer might earn 9 or 10 shillings a week, while the railway rate was between 3s and 5 shillings <u>a day</u>.*' (1)

42 year-old West Suffolk agricultural labourer Robert Crick, for example, earned nine shillings in one week in 1842. With his 40 year-old wife's wages and those of their three sons aged twelve, eleven and eight, their weekly income came to thirteen shillings and nine pence to feed themselves and two other children aged six and four. Robert Crick's money all went on buying bread; other expenditure for the week was for potatoes, tea, sugar, soap, blue, thread etc., candles, salt, coal and wood, butter, cheese and rent. All this amounted to exactly 13 shillings and 9 pence, so there was not even a halfpenny to spare. *(Stephen Denison, Enquiry into the Employment of Women and Children in Suffolk, Norfolk and*

Lincoln, Parliamentary Papers (1843)). (2) Robert Crick and his wife were in fact better housekeepers than most, as Stephen Denison observed:

There are numbers of families who, although in the possession of the amount of wages shown above, do not dispose of it with such frugality, but appear in the greatest state of destitution; many others, with the same number of children, do not get the wages this man's family have.' (3)

Whatever the reason, James Coultas made the decision to live in Suffolk and to work as a railway platelayer in or near Framlingham, not far distant from his sister Ann at Benhall. He and Eliza were living somewhere in Framlingham when their first child, Mary Betsy Coultas, was born on December 9th 1859, but their address is not known.

Interior of Parham Church, 2004, showing the font where Eliza Ann Coultas was christened in 1861. The octagonal font dates from the fifteenth century.

Framlingham, then as now, was an attractive market town with an historic castle, fine buildings and a large church with a tower 96 feet high, close to the Market Square. The origins of the castle are *'lost in obscurity'* (4) but go back well before it's rebuilding in the 12th century by a member of the Bigod family. It was to feature in the power struggle for the throne on the death of King Edward VI at the age of fifteen. Lady Jane Grey was proclaimed Queen on July 6th 1553, but support for her cause faded and thirteen days later it was announced that Mary, the daughter of Henry VIII and Catherine of Aragon, would become Queen. Mary ('Bloody Mary' as she came to be known) was staying at Framlingham Castle when she heard the news. White describes it as:

'one of the most magnificent and formidable baronial castles of the Saxon and Norman eras' (5) though it was reduced to a mere shell in about 1650, chiefly to build alms-houses and a workhouse under the will of Sir Robert Hitcham. Only the curtain wall with its thirteen towers remained. The Coultas family would surely have been to look at the castle and perhaps walked around its walls, although in those days they had a rather run-down appearance, being covered in ivy and with trees hiding much of the stonework. James and Eliza would have known well the names of Robert Hitcham and another wealthy benefactor, Thomas Mills, who died in 1703; even today they are both remembered, since two local schools are named after them.

By 1861, the year Queen Victoria's beloved husband Albert died from typhoid, James and Eliza had moved a short distance away to a new home in Church Street, Parham, where their second daughter, Eliza Ann, was born. She was christened in the church there on November 3rd 1861, in an octagonal font that dates from the early 15th century. Parham is a small village some 2½ miles from Framlingham, with its church just off the main road that runs past the village from the A12 to Framlingham. The church was built during the reign of Edward III (1327-77) and is even today in active use. Living in Church Street, the Coultas family must have seen regular comings and goings of churchgoers each week, and would no doubt have attended Sunday services themselves unless there was a good reason not to do so. From 1811 onwards at least, all the family's marriages and christenings appear to have been in church rather than chapel, so it is a fair assumption that the Coultases and the Allcocks belonged to the Church of England, as did a majority of those attending religious worship in Suffolk in 1851. According to John Glyde Junior's survey in *'Suffolk in the Nineteenth Century'*:

'It appears that the population of Suffolk on March 30th 1851 was three hundred and thirty-seven thousand two hundred and thirteen.' (cf. the figure quoted in *"A History of Suffolk"* above) *'Of this population there were, in the afternoon of that day, 136,820 persons attending public worship in 719 places. Of these...nearly two-thirds, 86,095, belonged to the Church of England.* [Others included Independents, Baptists, Methodists, Jews (only ten), Unitarians, Roman Catholics (374), Mormons and Friends] *'...A variety of circumstances necessarily prevent a large number of persons from attending public worship. A large deduction from the total population must be made on account of infants and young children, there being in Suffolk, in 1851, as many as 85,843 under ten years of age; 45,040 of this number were under five years. There will also always be a certain number absent from sickness, and a proportionate number kept at home as attendants and in charge of houses.*

The infirmities of age would cause another deduction. The number of persons in Suffolk, in 1851, aged seventy and upwards, was 12,846. Employment in connection with public conveyances, as railways, steamboats, coaches, cabs, etc., will produce another class of absentees from religious ordinances.'

This suggests that Eliza Coultas and Ann Allcock may have had to attend Church without their railway worker husbands on most occasions.

'Other minor causes exist, and Horace Mann, Esq., after a careful and elaborate review of what may be considered lawful impediments to attendance upon public worship, arrives at the conclusion that the accommodation requisite for those who are <u>able,</u> not merely those who are <u>willing,</u> to attend, should amount to 58 per cent. of the population. This estimate allows that 141,732 of our residents will, of necessity, be absent whenever divine service is performed, and that sittings in religious edifices in this county are not required for more than 195,583 persons.' (6)

The population of Parham village was falling steadily – from 532 in 1854 to 477 by 1874. (7) Two large estates dominated the local area; Parham Hall was the home of the Willoughby family (Parham's public house was the Willoughby Arms), while Parham New Hall was the seat of Frederick Snowden Corrance JP DL. It is described as

'a handsome mansion in the Grecian style, erected in 1851 on the site of Parham Lodge, upon a commanding eminence, surrounded by pleasure grounds.'

Parham Lodge had been the home of well-known Suffolk poet George Crabbe from 1793–1796, who had been born at Aldeburgh but moved from Parham to Great Glemham Hall after the loss of his son Edmund. Another notable parishioner had been Joshua Kirby FRS AS (1717–1774) who was born in Parham and became a topographical designer and designer in perspective to King George III. He was the son of John Kirby of Wickham Market, himself celebrated as the author of *'The Suffolk Traveller'* which was compiled from an actual survey of the county from 1732 to 1734.

Perhaps as they were growing up the Coultas children were told how in 1734 the bones of a man, an urn, and the head of a spear, were found in Parham in an old gravel pit and were supposed to have belonged to a Danish chieftain. They may have been intrigued to know that a small cannon ball had been dug up in the parish in 1853 and wondered how it had come to be there. Parham's vicarage house was relatively new when the Coultas family arrived, having been built in 1848 only eleven years earlier. Poor people in the village also benefited from two charitable bequests; in 1703 Thomas Mills had not only bequeathed money at Framlingham, but also left twenty shillings a year for distributions of bread in Parham, while Mrs Mary Warner gave £1.14 shillings worth of bread, and to the minister six shillings and eight pence for a sermon on Good Friday. She also gave an annuity of £5 for ten poor families of Parham who were not receiving parochial relief. (8) The village post office was run by Mr James Frost who was a joiner and builder as well as the postmaster. He would need to be an early riser and work quite late by today's standards; letters arrived at 4.55 am from Wickham Market and were despatched at 8.45 pm. Framlingham, in the opposite direction, was the nearest money order office.

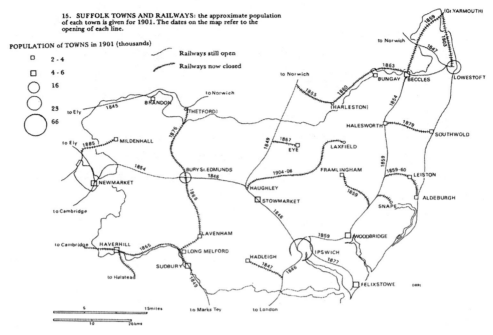

Map of Suffolk Towns and Railways, showing East Suffolk Line and the Framlingham Branch Line opened in 1859. Isaac Allcock and James Coultas would have worked on these lines.

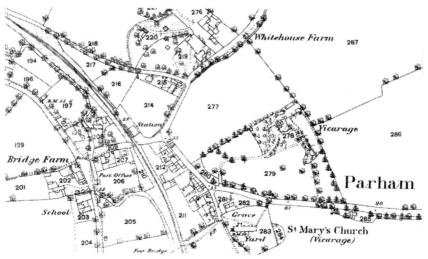

Map of Parham showing the station and the railway line, 1883.

Parham Railway Station, with Signal Box and Post office on the right of the picture, circa 1900. The ford and bridge across the river Ore can be seen in the foreground. The single track railway ran (from right to left) from Wickham Market (Campsea Ashe) to Framlingham.

A railway line ran through the middle of Parham village to Framlingham, part of the East Suffolk branch of the Great Eastern Railway which was under construction in 1859. The village boasted a fairly grand station house and the station master at the time was a Mr William Baldry. It seems fairly certain that James Coultas was recruited to work as a platelayer on this branch line and others nearby when he moved to Suffolk and came to live in Parham.

The age of the railway had begun with the opening of the Stockton & Darlington line as early as 1825, and by 1850 throughout the country there were some 7,500 miles of track. First activity on the Great Eastern Railway (GER) tracks came on June 18th 1836 when two trains, each with a locomotive fore and aft, proceeded parallel to each other along the 5-foot gauge double track from a temporary terminus at Mile End to another temporary structure at Romford. Guns were fired in salute and guests were entertained by the band of the Coldstream Guards. Financial problems and disputes with landowners meant that there was a seven-year delay until the line could reach Colchester, in 1843. (9) As with any new invention, railways brought with them fear and concern; many landowners objected to the damage to the countryside, the loss of valuable agricultural and common land, and disturbance to their animals, birds and crops. They feared for their pheasant and partridge shooting and fox hunting, and were alarmed that their cattle and sheep would suffer from these new-fangled machines. It would be another three years before the railway lines crossed the Essex and Suffolk border and reached Ipswich.

There were 'railway booms' in 1836–37 and again in 1845–48, but the development of the rail network was really a continuous process and not fully complete until the end of the century. (10) John Glyde recorded that in 1851, the county of Suffolk had fifty-two railway engine drivers and stokers, ten of them being under twenty years of age. There were also 162 Railway Labourers, and 199 *'others engaged in railway traffic'.* (11) Needless to say, none of them was a woman. The 1851 Census for the whole country listed 65,000 males in the category of 'railway driver, etc., porter, etc., labourer, platelayer', but in the same category, females numbered only fifty four. (12).

As David Dymond and Peter Northeast make clear in *'A History of Suffolk'*:

'Although the industry and commerce of Suffolk had benefited from the improved roads and navigations of the eighteenth century, the coming of the railways to the county in the 1840s and 1850s had an even greater effect. The towns of Ipswich and Bury St Edmunds were linked by rail to London in 1846, Lowestoft to Norwich in 1847 and to Ipswich in 1859, and Sudbury to London in 1849. As a result these towns all grew and attracted new industry, especially Ipswich where the new wet dock, also built in the 1840s, allowed modern ships right up to the town. The extension of the railway to Suffolk's seaside resorts – Aldeburgh in 1860, Felixstowe in 1877 and Southwold, by the famous narrow-gauge line, in 1879 – brought them appreciably more visitors and trade.' (13, and see *Map of Suffolk Towns and Railways, page 19*).

Such increases, however, meant that traffic on the roads was considerably reduced. James Hissey, giving an account of *'A Tour in a Phaeton'* in 1889, illustrates the peace and tranquillity of the East Suffolk countryside following the introduction of railways:

'A short distance from Wickham Market we noticed a five-fingered sign-post…all the arms were in excellent condition, the inscriptions on each being perfectly legible; would that all sign-posts were as serviceable to the traveller as this! But then in these railway days who ever dreams of going any distance by road…?

'As we proceeded along we presently came to the Lion Inn, evidently a decayed coaching house, and looking now sadly desolate in its fallen estate, doing duty as a roadside public. We were on the main high road from London to Yarmouth, erst busy with much traffic and musical with the sound of the frequent coach-horn. Now we had the way all to ourselves; since we left Woodbridge we had met no vehicle of any kind, and the one or two people we did see appeared to be farm labourers going to or from their work. Sadly deserted are the old high roads, amongst the most lonely in the land.

'Then on through shady woods our way led us to a very pretty little hamlet, the name of which was not given on our map; the village school here [Benhall] with its yellow thatched roof and quaint bell turret tempted us to pull up and make a sketch…'

'We made our midday halt at Saxmundham, a quiet little market-town…looking now, doubtless, much as it did a century ago, and as in all probability it will look a century hence. A slumberous town that wakes up into some semblance of activity one day in seven, when the market is held there, and farmers and their wives jog in from the country round to do a little business and a good deal of gossip'. (14) If only this part of the road from Ipswich to Lowestoft and Great Yarmouth, now the A12, was as quiet and free from traffic

today as it was in 1889.

Railways were also a major factor in encouraging people to leave Suffolk. For example, David Dymond and Peter Northeast note that '*at Orford in 1861, a decrease of population was attributed to families in the fishing trade moving with the opening of the railway.*' The only decade in which the population of the county actually declined was 1851–61, as the network of major lines was completed. (15) In this respect at least, the Allcock and Coultas families, by moving into Suffolk from Nottinghamshire, were helping to stem the tide.

Passenger trains came into Framlingham station from 1859 until 1952.

The first trains to run from Yarmouth and Lowestoft to Ipswich were decorated with evergreens. The local press welcomed the service and a report read: '*trains run with great punctuality, and all are loud in their praises of the excellence of the line, and the commodiousness of the new carriages and stations*'. With connections available to London, cheap trips to the capital began every Friday. (16)

In 1858, *The Post Office Directory of Suffolk* records the near completion of the East Suffolk branch line through Parham, although local people were looking forward to it with varying degrees of enthusiasm. The entry for Framlingham reads: '*The East Suffolk railway line will be opened early in the year, with the branch, from the main line at Campsey Ashe to a commodious terminus, at the entrance of the town to the south, where already great improvements have been made preparatory for the occasion.*' For Parham, the entry is straightforward: '*The East Suffolk Railway, now in course of completion, passes through this parish and has a station here.*' The Wickham Market comment on the other hand is more grudging, since its residents had discovered that the splendid new branch line would bypass the town itself completely: '*Much of the traffic has been taken off the road by railways now running, and the remainder is soon likely to follow in consequence of the approaching opening of the East Suffolk railway, which passes without entering the town; the nearest station to Wickham Market it is expected will be at Camprey Ash [sic] a village two miles from the town.'* (17)

Once the railway was finished, Framlingham would have a station master who would live on the upper floor of the station. Downstairs were the waiting rooms, booking office, and toilets. (18) Trevor May shows that at larger stations across the country the station master would be *'a man of some substance'*, perhaps wearing *'a frock coat and silk hat for special occasions – a sure sign of his middle-class status. Joseph Pascoe wrote of the station master in 1878: it would be difficult to state at what time of the day his duties commence, and at what time they are completed. At any hour of the night he was likely to be woken from his sleep in order to deal with some emergency.'* (19) However, in small rural villages the situation could be entirely different: *'for example Wanstrow station near Frome in Somerset was the smallest station on the Great Western Railway, and it had no staff of its own. On winter days in the Edwardian era, when five trains a day in each direction stopped there, it was a platelayer* [such as James Coultas] *who would light the station-room fire and see to the lamps in the evening.'* (20) Parham did have a station master but probably few if any staff, so James could well have been asked to help out with similar duties at the station on occasion.

"The rules and regulations of the London & Great North Western (Railway) in 1849 (and no doubt those for the Great Eastern at Framlingham would have been similar) *included the following instructions for station masters:*

He is to take care that all the servants at his Station come on duty clean in their persons and clothes, shaved, and with their shoes brushed.

He is also to cause the Station to be kept clear of weeds, and have the ballast raked and preserved in neat order. He must be careful that all stores supplied for the Station are prudently and economically used, and that there is no waste of gas, oil, coal or stationery." (21)

The grand opening of the line from Wickham Market (Campsea Ashe) to Framlingham, via Marlesford and Parham, was held on June 1st 1859. As an inspector, Isaac Allcock could well have been on duty for the celebrations, and James Coultas, newly arrived in Suffolk, might have been there too. Church bells were rung throughout the day, a cricket match was played and teas were provided at Framlingham's Crown Hotel, but there was a problem when a porter fell in front of a train. Luckily the driver was able to stop his engine before any serious injury was done but, since the porter was also the leader of the town band, the concert to celebrate the opening had to be cancelled. (22)

The branch line through Parham, over five miles in length, was built at an estimated cost of just over £40,000 and initially the weekday service was four trains each way daily and two on Sundays. Railway companies were required by the Railway Act of 1844 to provide a minimum service of one train a day each way, travelling at not less than twelve miles per hour and stopping at every passenger station, charging no more than 1d. per mile for third class passengers. The line, despite all the excitement at its opening, was less well used than had been hoped; its passenger traffic was generally poor, although when

Framlingham College (an independent school built under royal charter as the Suffolk memorial to Prince Albert and still in existence today) was opened in 1864, there were fluctuating increases. Yet Framlingham did become an important railhead, with the station a major grain despatch point. (23)

Valerie Porter paints a picture of changing life in places such as Framlingham or Parham where there was a Victorian country station: '*Many a villager enjoyed the simple pleasure of watching the evening train come in, and the station bridge became another focal point where people could meet casually and chat. The station also became a centre for means of communications other than trains. The electric telegraph system, by which messages concerning railway matters were passed down the line to other stations, was soon used to pass messages on behalf of the post office with the station master acting as agent for postal telegrams…The combination of telegraph and railway became a means of spreading information about job opportunities elsewhere, tempting workers away from the villages. The railways also introduced a new concept of time. Before, everything had happened slowly and time was relative: people kept local time, regardless of what time it was thought to be elsewhere. There had been no need to conform to other people's schedules until the railway network demanded standardization for its timetables. Gradually villagers came to accept 'railway' time (Greenwich time) throughout the country and everyone who had a clock could set it to coincide with everyone else's.*' (24)

Railway platelayers like James Coultas, the men who laid and looked after the railway tracks, tended to stay in one place only for a limited time. As Trevor May indicates, '*Gangers and platelayers had the task of maintaining the track once it had been laid*', (25) but once a line was completed, it would need only a relatively limited amount of maintenance, so most of the workers would then move on to a new stretch of line. This may account for why James and Eliza seem to have lived in four different places in rural East Suffolk, quite close to each other, in the space of about fourteen years. '*In the 1880s the Great Northern Railway had a thousand platelayers on the line between London and Edinburgh, earning wages of between £1 and £1.10s a week*', (26) though earnings in Suffolk might well have been less than this. Platelayers '*were out in all weathers repairing the track and laying fog signals when required, so not surprisingly, they had the highest accident rate of all railwaymen*'. (27) Towards the end of his life, James was given additional responsibility and became a foreman platelayer but then changed his occupation again to become a railway gate-keeper. This might have been due to ill health or injury as gate keeping would have been a less physically demanding job. It would however have needed a cool head and attention to duty, ensuring that the gates opened and closed in good time for the trains to pass safely, keeping the gates well lit and making sure that pedestrian and horse traffic were well clear of the line when required.

There would have been many rules and instructions for James to obey, with breaches of rules bringing with them the fear of a fine or even dismissal. As Trevor May records: '*In 1873 the Railway Service Gazette carried a piece entitled 'The Railwayman's*

Ten Commandments', *which included such injunctions as 'Honour thy official and carry tales' and* *'thou shalt commit 300 rules to memory.'* (28) Presumably this was a light-hearted look at the orders railwaymen were expected to follow, and the instruction to 'carry tales' was the equivalent of 'whistle-blowing' today. There were some 'perks' however, to benefit families such as the Coultases and the Allcocks, including *'cheap coal, free* *clothing, company housing, relative security and the prospect of a pension.'* (29)

Chapter Four

Family Life

Between 1863 and 1871 Eliza Coultas gave birth to several more babies. Home for the family was now nearer to Benhall, in the village of Farnham, where my grandmother Susannah was born on August 18th 1863 and christened in the parish church. Ann and Isaac Allcock had mourned the death of a second child the previous year when John George had died at Benhall in February 1862, only two months old. Before long however Ann was pregnant again, and soon after Susannah was born, her aunt and uncle were able to rejoice in the birth of their youngest son, Charles Marshall Allcock. He was born at Benhall on October 15th 1863. If the families were at all superstitious, they would have had plenty of 'secrets' to 'communicate to the bees' at this time in their lives.

Childbearing was a constant feature of life at this time; many women spent about twelve years of married life either pregnant or breastfeeding. Birth control was neither a realistic nor an acceptable option. As Judith Flanders notes in 'The Victorian House', 'women had an average of 5.5 births (although somewhat fewer children were born alive), with 80% of women having their first child within a year of marriage'. (1) While middle-class expectant mothers were exhorted to take care of themselves for the sake of the baby, Cassell's Household Guide of 1869–71 emphasised that this could not apply to working-class women:

'We know that it is utterly impossible for the wife of a labouring man to give up work and what is called 'take care of herself', as others can. Nor is it necessary. 'The back is made for its burthen'. It would be just as injurious for the labourer's wife to give up her daily work, as for the lady to take to sweeping her own carpets or cooking the dinner'. (2)

Dr Lori Williamson, in her paper on health and medicine in the nineteenth-century countryside, shows that 'few could afford to pay a country doctor's fees, although many physicians treated their patients free of charge.' (3) Villagers had for the most part to depend on goodwill from the community where medical help and midwifery were concerned:

'In general, self-help and self-sufficiency formed the basis of rural medical care. Neighbours would rely upon each other for assistance, and doctors would be called only once all home remedies had failed or when the patient was close to death. For a modest fee of a couple of shillings, the village midwife, who possessed neither anaesthetics nor obstetrical instruments and who received her training on the job...would assist a woman in labour; a doctor would attend a birth only if there were severe complications...Charity also played its part in post-natal care.

The new village mother would receive from the clergyman's daughter "the box", which contained baby clothes on loan and gifts of tea, sugar and groats for gruel. "The box" would be returned to the rectory after one month, with the contents cleaned and ready for the next arrival.' (4)

Hodskinson's Map of Suffolk in 1783 – extract showing the area of East Suffolk where James and Eliza Coultas and their family lived and worked. Apart from the coming of the railway, the rural nature of the area would have changed little by the mid-1800s.

After the birth of three daughters, James and Eliza must have longed for a boy, and their first son was christened Robert Haythorne Coultas at Farnham on December 24th 1865. Christmas, one of the few times in the year when Victorian cottagers might be able to take a holiday and break from work, must have been extra special that year. Two more girls followed – Sarah Mabel Coultas born on January 6th 1868 and christened at Farnham Church on March 15th and Louisa Charlotte Coultas, born on December 9th 1869 and christened at the church on January 30th 1870.

When James and Eliza were bringing up their family in Farnham it was a peaceful spot; apart from the coming of the railways, the quiet rural nature of the area had probably changed little since Joseph Hodskinson produced his *Map of Suffolk* in 1783. (5) [See page 28]. *Morris's Directory of Suffolk* for 1868 describes Farnham as:

'opposite Stratford St Andrew, the river Alde dividing the villages' (6), but in contrast today it stands on a bend of the busy main A12 road with constant traffic streaming past the two villages, so it is possible to fail to notice the river. In 1874, 172 people lived in Farnham but population numbers had been falling, like those at Parham, from 216 in 1801 and 1831, and again to 195 by 1851. The parish church is a fairly plain one in the Norman style with a flint tower and set on a small hill. It is one of the few churches that still contains Georgian box pews, as it would have done when the Coultas family were there. The incumbent was the Rev Henry Thompson BA, who was able to live in a brand new residence built by the patron and Lord of the Manor William Long in 1869. Perhaps Susannah with Robert and Sarah Mabel watched as it was being built. Living in Farnham at the time were farmers, two butchers, a thrashing (*sic*) machine proprietor, a horse and cattle dealer and a sheep skin and coal dealer. George Nicholds was one of two grocers and drapers as well as the village sub-postmaster; on weekdays letters came from Wickham Market at 8 am (9 am on Sundays) and were dispatched at 6.15 pm. (7) With the introduction of the Penny Post from 1840, the village shop and post office, often combined, would have been an important hub of village life. As the Rev Richard Cobbold observed of Wortham's village shop in his survey of that Suffolk parish in 1860,

'Here all the villagers go to post their letters for the Post Office is here established! Here, also, the paupers of the parish go to receive the liberal dole of the poor Laws, donations, grants, or merciful considerations of the poor rates. Here also the Relieving Officer meets them, and they receive their flour and their pence.' (8)

No doubt Farnham's George & Dragon Inn (formerly The George), where Thomas Pearse was the licensee, was also well frequented by the locals in the village and maybe by James himself.

In a compact village such as Farnham, most people would know each other and take more than a passing interest in their affairs. If (as happened even in the 1930s and 1940s in the village where I grew up) a child was seen 'scrumping' apples from a neighbour's tree, someone passing would be sure to report it to his parents and there was a near certainty that the miscreant would be caned as a result. If a candle was seen glowing in a cottage at one o'clock in the morning, by the next day most people would know a new infant had been born or someone had died. When a confused old lady accidentally fell into the village pond, it would be talked about for months. The impending arrival of a new rector or curate was a cause for endless speculation and concern. People tended to gather to gossip or to meet together socially to give themselves some relief from the daily round. As Valerie Porter says in *'English Villagers-Life in the Countryside'*:

'In a life of relentless hard work, which bound the villagers together in one way, shared social activities were equally important in cementing the community. There was little artificial division between work and play: both were part of the life of the village and took place largely within it. Entertainments – to lift people's hearts a little, if not necessarily their minds and souls – were generated by the villagers themselves, providing a rich mixture of activities to fill such brief leisure hours as there might be. The simplest was the traditional Sunday evening stroll down the village street, after Church or chapel, to see and be seen, to pass the time of day, to make your face familiar and to remind other villagers of your existence.' (9)

A marriage in the parish would also be a noteworthy event. Rev Cobbold describes such an occasion at one of the cottages in Wortham:

'What a lonely lost cottage this appears to be and yet in this very cottage I was at as happy a marriage feast as I ever saw…The bride asked me if I should be on the Long Green at one o'clock to call and say 'Grace' for her at her feast. To say Grace is to ask for the blessing of God or offer a thankful heart for the gifts of his abundance.

'I went, I said Grace, and just as I was about to carve the plum-pudding the bride rose – and came with a plate to me with these words: 'Pray, Sir, would you be so good as to cut the first slice for my Father in Law, who is at work in Mr Cullingford's Barn and cannot come until the evening? – I will just run across with it to him and will soon be back again.'

Such happiness in mid-Victorian times however was all too often tinged with sadness just around the corner, as Richard Cobbold goes on to show: *'Yet have I lived to see that bride tend that husband on his death-bed, and herself a widow with one little boy – and often in our Sunday School have I noticed the child and often endeavoured to comfort the Mother.*

> *Thus in a lonely cot I virtue knew,*
> *But all things here are transient and fade*
> *God takes away. He has his ends in view*
> *No man his will can, if he would, evade.'* (10)

One very familiar figure in Farnham would have been the parish clerk, Amos Newson, who was born in 1824 and held the office of Clerk, for both Farnham and Stratford St Andrew, for some fifty-five years. He must have played a significant role in parish and church life and would surely have been well known to James and Eliza Coultas. His job was an important one, particularly in the earlier part of the nineteenth century, as shown by Katherine Doughty's obituary for another long serving parish clerk in Suffolk from 1823–1892, William Pipe:

There have been many changes during seventy years, and when first appointed in succession to his father, he was doubtless a far greater man than he was at his death. Few of his class then could read, and he was truly the voice of the people, as he led them through prayer and psalm, speaking slowly, and in the Suffolk dialect which they all could follow. Now the responses are said by the choir, but there are a few old people, survivors of those unlettered days, who stand with vacant eyes and bookless hands, lost without a guiding voice they had learned so well to understand.

"The Church will never feel itself without him", they say, and it certainly does not look itself. He made a picture sitting in his carved seat below the reading desk, a large prayer book open before him, and the light from a south window falling on his snowy hair and lion-like face, revered with age. When he stood he was taller than most of the congregation, and leaned forward his face lighted with pleasure, as his musical old voice started the chants and hymns.' (11)

Amos Newson, with his wife Elizabeth and their two children Louisa and Thomas, who both predeceased them, are buried in the churchyard at Farnham where their gravestone survives to this day.

It is not known where, if at all, the Coultas children went to school while they were in Suffolk but there were various possible options depending on where they were living at the time. *'A History of Suffolk'* notes that;

Until the establishment of Board Schools after 1870, education was entirely in the hands of voluntary bodies...By 1833, 187 places in Suffolk had schools for poor children, attended by over 8,000 pupils – approximately 22% of the child population. After the introduction of government grants in 1833, the number of schools increased steadily, so that by 1870 over 400 schools were open in 374 different places, with accommodation for about 37,500 children, or 60% of the children in Suffolk.' (12)

Forster's Education Act of 1870 required local authorities to provide education by setting up partially funded Board Schools in places where existing provision was inadequate. Schooling would have been free to poor families but for others there would be a weekly fee. It was not until the 1880 Elementary Act, unless there were local by-laws to this effect, that education became compulsory for children under the age of ten.

The Allcock children would almost certainly have received schooling in the village of Benhall where they lived. Benhall was little more than a mile from Farnham, but larger and more widely scattered. In 1871 it had 151 inhabited houses and only two uninhabited, housing a total of 644 people. The parish included Benhall Street, Silver Lace Green and Benhall Green, and in fact had more than one school with about 100 pupils between them. Benhall had benefited from a legacy from Sir Edward Duke as long ago as 1731, whereby £1000 was to be settled for the support of a schoolmaster to teach poor children of the parish to read, write and learn arithmetic. Part of the legacy was spent on a new master's house and school, playground and garden. In 1868 this was known as the Free School, with Mr D Reynolds as the master and Miss Mary B Reynolds (who may have been his sister or daughter) as the sewing mistress. There was also a Benhall Street School, where Mrs Sarah Mills was the mistress and an Infant School, whose mistress was Mrs Susannah Gooding. Miss Frances Fryett, previously of Farnham, was also teaching there in 1874. (13)

School for the Coultases at this time could also have been at Benhall; it is unlikely to have been in Farnham itself. According to *'Suffolk Parish History'* compiled by Suffolk County Council, the village had only a Sunday School in 1818 and just a small infant school with ten pupils in 1833. No school is listed there in 1874 (14) and by 1891 Farnham scholars went either to Benhall or Stratford St Andrew. Stratford's school was new in 1865 and by 1891 it had 53 pupils attending, so they may also have gone there.

The school day would probably have started around 9 am and finished at 4.30 pm, with time off for a meal. The children would have been expected to walk home and back for their midday meal unless they lived too far away. The village school-room would have been quite small and plain, perhaps with Christian tracts or samplers and a picture of Queen Victoria on the walls. Different age groups would often be taught together, with the use of blackboards and chalk, copy books or slates. Wooden benches or desks, a cupboard and perhaps a small coal-burning stove may well have completed the scene. A description of one such school found its way into an 1874 Annual of *'Good Things for the Young of All Ages'*:

The village school was held in a thatched cottage upon the village common, and there was always such a musical hum coming from the door, it was like a hive of bees. If you peeped in as you went by, you would be sure to see a number of children as busy as bees over their lessons and their sums. There they sat in two rows before the open door – the biggest behind – with the sunshine bringing out all the rich browns and golden shades in the little lowered heads; but sometimes a ray would point at a disconsolate small drone on a form or in a corner. This, however, was seldom the case now…'

Emphasis was placed on teaching the basic subjects of reading, spelling, writing and arithmetic, while the girls may also have been taught home-making skills such as needlework that would be useful to them in later life, whether they were to become servants or housewives with families of their own. The school may have had a system of monitoring in place, whereby older pupils assisted the teacher by helping the younger children with some of their lessons. Although this practice came to be frowned upon, it was still alive and well in the Second World War at my first private school in Guildford in the 1940s. With many young teachers away because of the war effort, I was called upon as an eight year old to help younger pupils aged five and six with their reading and sums, and the Coultas and Allcock children may well have done the same. Their playground games in the mid-1800s would no doubt have included blind man's buff, leap-frog, hopscotch and tug of war. Marbles, hoops and sticks and home made spinning tops would have been very popular too.

By 1871, James and Eliza and their young family had yet another new home – their fourth since coming to Suffolk. On the Census for that year, they were to be found living in Brick Lane, Framlingham, a narrow track with fields on either side that runs between Parham and Framlingham, close to Coles Green. It is not possible today to identify the cottage where they lived, but on the Census of 1901 the only address listed in Brick Lane is Railway Gate House, so it seems likely that this was the home of James Coultas, who is described as a railway gate-keeper towards the end of 1873.

All the Coultas children, with the exception of baby Louisa Charlotte, are shown on the 1871 Census as 'scholars', so presumably by then at least they were enrolled as school pupils somewhere in the area. Living in Brick Lane at this time, they may have gone to school in Framlingham or, more probably to Parham as it was a little nearer and the family had lived there before. Parham had a Church School built in 1841 with the support of Mr Frederick Corrance, the patron, and designed to educate some forty poor children of the parish. By 1871, however, new school buildings were needed; these were paid for through voluntary contributions and aided by government grant. The foundation stone for the new village school was laid in 1872 by Charles Corrance who was just nine at the time. Tragically, within three years he had died. Running of the school was in the hands of the Parham School Committee and minutes of their meetings from 1872, at the time the Coultas children may have been pupils there, give interesting insights into the 'teething troubles' that had to be addressed.

The School Trust Deed required *'the principal officiating minister for the time being to have the religious & moral instruction of all the scholars attending such school...'* and to be the chairman of the committee. The Rev Charles T Corrance MA as incumbent of Parham Church therefore became chairman, with eight other committee members, not all of whom attended on every occasion. Minutes of their first meeting on April 23rd 1872 refer to *'a meeting of ratepayers about a fortnight previous* (which had made decisions) *to the effect that:*

The school should be opened (if possible) the 5th day of May under Pamela Rackham, who was appointed for 6 mo. from that date at salary of £25 per an. – the appointment to be subject to reconsideration.

...it was resolved that on the basis of the following estimate of expenses, a rate of 4d.in the pound be made on the parish:

half yrs salary for Mistress	*12.10.0d*
half yrs salary for assistant teacher	*4.00.0d*
Furnishing	*20.00.0d*
Roll blinds	*2.00.0d*
School appliances	*6.00.0d*
Total	*£44.10.0d*

The School fees for the present be the same as under the old School – namely 1d per week for each pupil.

Mr Gray and Mr Revitt be requested to undertake the furnishing of the house.'

On June 2nd there were four resolutions:

'that Mr Gray be empowered to purchase a clock to the value of £.1, and a work table with drawers; that Mr Frost (presumably the one who was the joiner, builder and village postmaster) *be instructed to make a case for the books, also to paint and varnish board and make stand for same; that Mr Gray be requested* ('instructed' was crossed out!) *to have the furniture which he had purchased to the value of £, (sic) put into the house within 14 days';* and that *'as certain complaints had been made to the Schoolmistress by the parents – they should in future be referred to some member or some meeting of the Committee and that no such complaints be listened to by the mistress.'*

The chairman was absent from the meeting on June 16th, held at 7pm, but a Mr D Smithers was *'called to the chair'* for several important items of business:

The Minutes of the preceding meeting having been read, the furniture & school appliances were inspected and approved of. The table had not been bought & on reconsideration was considered superfluous.

'It was resolved that the room be cleaned by the elder girls who should be chosen in twos by the mistress to take their turn weekly, those in office to be exempted from payment of fees.

'It was resolved that the regulation fee be 1d. per head on all children attending. That exceptions in which a higher or a lower fee might be desirable be adjudicated on severally & individually by the Committee.'

Various decisions were made on this crucial issue, ranging from no lower fee being allowed to a higher charge of 2d. for seven pupils and permission for two children to attend for a joint fee of 3d.

The meeting on July 28th was poorly attended, with only three members present, and the minutes show that the committee had run into some problems:

'Complaint was made to the Committee that the girls instructed to clean the room had refused & some of them had been withdrawn by the parents. The members present undertook to see the respective parents & endeavour that the said scholars should clean the room till the close of the term.

'Complaint was made by the mistress respecting Mrs Mayhew for hitting one of the scholars on the school premises. D Smith offered to investigate this.

'It was resolved that the term do close on Aug. 15 for the month's vacation.

'This day was subsequently altered by private arrangement to the 8th.'

On September 6th there were more members present and they agreed that the present scale of fees should continue. They were also determined to get tough on disobedience:

'It was resolved that 6 boys or girls be selected by the schoolmistress to clean the school room daily by turn – their fees to be remitted for their service – Any refusal to perform the duty to be punished by dismissal.'

At the same time as they were wielding the 'stick' they were able to produce a 'carrot':

'An offer on the part of Fredk Corrance Esq to give the scholars and their parents a fete on his grounds was cordially accepted by the Committee & the date was fixed for the 23rd inst.'

Probably because of other commitments especially during harvest time, the committee decided to change to quarterly meetings and the first of these was held at 10 am on the school premises on September 30th 1873. The committee authorised the Rev C T Corrance *'to purchase for the use of the school:*

1½ dozen Murby's Introductory primer – 68 pp. price 6d.

1½ dozen Spelling Books for Stand I

1½ dozen Spelling Books for Stand II

Alphabet in large letters for infants

One box of slate pencils & one box of chalks for the Black Board.'

In addition, a broken window in the school room was to be mended, and the school yards and garden were to be put in proper order as soon as convenient.

At future meetings members continued to discuss school business and make decisions. Frederick Snowden Corrance, Suffolk Magistrate and Deputy Lieutenant of the County, had by now joined the committee. This landowner, with property in London and at Broadwater, Framlingham as well as Parham New Hall, appears to have taken on many positions of responsibility in the county and worked tirelessly on behalf of the local community. He may well have been regarded as 'into everything'. Committee resolutions included giving Joshua Rackham (who just happened to be the father of schoolmistress Pamela) the refusal, which he accepted, of the school garden to cultivate and keep it tidy; ordering of 3 tuns of coal with kindling for the annual consumption of the school house and grounds and ordering that the class room fireguard should be repaired and a new one ordered for the large school room. School chimnies (*sic*) required attention. Most importantly for Pamela Rackham,

'It was resolved that a Special Meeting should be called for the election of a school mistress, so soon as the result of her recent examination for a certificate in London is made known.'

The chairman of the school committee duly received a letter from the Education Department in Whitehall London dated 28th March 1874 with the good news that Pamela had passed her examination and had obtained a place in the Third Division of the Class List. In May therefore she was offered a salary for May 5th 1874 to May 5th 1875 of £35 per annum, and

'one moiety of any government grant which may be earned during the above period.'

At the same time, the committee decided to raise the school fees paid by all the parents by another penny in addition to the existing amount. This was just as well, since the treasurer had to report three months later that the total amount collected from May 1873 to May 1874 was £50.0.4d., whereas the amount expended during the same period was £51.12.1¼d. The school then had a visit from a government inspector who recommended more change of books for each class; no doubt this would have increased expenditure still further. (15)

If and when they were not in school, the Allcock and Coultas children could well have been out at work, even from an early age. John Glyde, in his *'Suffolk in the Nineteenth Century'*, researched the situation of young people in the area in 1851:

'A very large number of children are employed at farm labour in this county. Both sexes are sent to the fields early in life to add to the scanty income of the family. John Pearson, Esq., of Framlingham, says: "Every person in the parish employ children in crow-keeping. I dare say at one time we had 50 or 60 children employed in crow-keeping'. In Hartismere, Hoxne, Woodbridge, Plomesgate (16), and Blything Unions, children are very generally employed…Mr Lane of Framlingham testified that children sometimes go to work at six years of age, they usually go at seven. In many districts, however, nine and ten years of age are most common to commence work.

The kind of work in which they are engaged varies in different districts. They are generally engaged in weeding, corn-dropping, pulling turnips, crow-keeping, and assist in stone picking, and, except in cases of scrofulous children, injurious effects on the health or constitution of children are seldom observed…

'Girls assist their mothers in stone-picking etc. at an early age, and in keeping birds. They are in some districts more employed than boys, and the elder girls so employed are sometimes absent from school from six to eight months in the year. Girls of sixteen generally earn 6d. a day…It may be safely affirmed that whatever the work of the locality might be, young children are forced to take their share in it, and to give up the real seed time of their education for a premature and unreasonable harvest…' (17)

Fifteen year old Hannah Winkup, born at Sibton, near Yoxford, into a family of twelve children, gave the following account to John Glyde of the work she had to undertake:

'…went out to work when I was twelve – keeping birds, sheep or cows; I frequently done boy's work – keeping sheep or cows is to prevent their getting into cornfields. I had 3d. a day; worked Sunday as well, but my master used to give me a dinner on Sunday. Have gone stone picking, haymaking, weeding and dropping. Earnt 5d a day at dropping; like hay making best. Stone-picking is the hardest work I done… I worked from eight o'clock in the morning to six o'clock in the evening. Got my breakfast before I went; was allowed one hour for dinner, from twelve to one; had no more until I went home at six. I had bread and cheese for breakfast and cold coffee, no sugar – same for dinner, and very often the same for supper.

At other times mother would boil a dumpling for us for supper, this was in stone-picking time, when we always come home very cold. We were so poor that sometimes I have had to go to bed without a supper; generally had a piece of meat on Sundays not butcher's meat, but pork.' (18)

There was a great deal of stone picking in the fields of Suffolk at this time, initially to protect the farm implements and horses and clean the land to improve the crops, but later so that the stones could be used for road and rail building and maintenance. As Hannah Winkup makes clear, it was a thankless, back-breaking task for little reward.

Although there would have been little money to spare, life in 1871 at Brick Lane must have seemed full of hope for James and Eliza Coultas. Work was available on the railways for James, while his wife was content to be at home and look after her growing family, or perhaps join the workers in the fields between confinements. She would have been busy preparing meals for the family; probably an early breakfast before work or school, dinner at midday with '*beaver*' in the afternoon (a snack mostly for farm workers) (19) followed by supper when James and the children arrived home for the evening. Mrs Beeton's celebrated book of '*Household Management*' had been published just ten years before, but although Eliza may have heard of it, it was unlikely to have had much impact on the way she looked after her family in their small rural home. In '*Eating with the Victorians*', C Anne Wilson says that:

'*A hot supper forming the main meal of a typical working family might consist of a little meat or fried bacon accompanied by potatoes or cabbage, carrots or turnips grown in the family's own small garden. For the better off there was bread and butter or a plain pudding in addition. But where the workplace was close to home, allowing the family to have their dinner as their main meal at the end of the morning, that was the substantial hot meal, and supper was smaller, comprising bread and cheese, or bread and butter, or potatoes.*' (20)

While Eliza would probably have used the village shop for basic provisions, she might also rely on people calling in with things to sell or collecting things she needed from farther afield. According to Valerie Porter in '*English Villagers*' the traditional method of shopping for:

'*occasional goods in rural areas was to acquire them direct from village craftsmen and producers, or to walk to the nearest weekly town market or a fair, or to make use of an assortment of itinerant traders who regularly called round the villages over the weeks and months, or to use the village carrier.*' (21)

The village of Farnham did have a carrier in 1868; (22) a Mr Edmonds went through to Ipswich each Tuesday and Friday, and returned the following day. By 1874 Benhall had at least two carriers passing through; (23) Cordell from Kelsale and Curtis from Halesworth, who also travelled to Ipswich on a Tuesday and a Friday.

Valerie Porter shows the importance of these delivery services at the time:

'*The carrier, with his horsedrawn tilt-cart or covered wagon, was the main link between village and town. He often began the service as an offshoot to a main trade which already involved him in the regular transportation of his own goods to market…Carriers took village goods to market on their producers' behalf and brought back goods for those who ordered them from town, be they huge boxes or a packet of pins or a collected debt. And there were 'egglers' or 'higglers' who went round the local farms and cottages collecting eggs, poultry, butter and similar produce to sell in town.*

'*Most villagers had neither the time nor inclination to travel to town themselves as shoppers but carriers often fitted rough benches as seats for those who wanted to make the trip. The number of carriers grew considerably during Victorian times and by the 1880s (when only one in six villages had its own railway station) there were at least 200,000 of them.'* (24)

Eliza would have expected the children to help out with daily chores at home. The 1874 *Good Things Annual,* in a series of *'Cottage Songs for Cottage Children'*, gives hints with appropriate illustrations on looking after the baby, sweeping the floor, drawing water, cleaning the windows and, as shown here, washing the clothes:

'This is the way we wash the clothes!
See the dirt and smoke and clay:
Through and through the water flows,
Takes and drops them far away.

This is the way we bleach the clothes:
Lay them out upon the green;
Through and through the sunshine goes–
Makes them white as well as clean.

This is the way we dry the clothes;
Hang them on the bushes about;
Through and through the soft wind blows,
Draws and drives the wetness out.

Water, sun and windy air,
Makes the clothes all clean and sweet;
Lay them now in lavender,
For the Sunday, folded neat."

When there was no school or work to be done, the Coultas children must have enjoyed playing with friends and their cousins in the fields, going for walks in the countryside or just catching tiddlers in the local streams. There would be wild flowers such as spring time primroses and cowslips to be picked, a variety of birds to see and butterflies to catch. My grandmother Susannah used to speak with fondness of visits to the hamlet of Snape Bridge on the River Alde, some three or four miles from Farnham. Writing in 1874, William White describes the Bridge (which had been built in 1802) as a good one, with:

'a commodious wharf and warehouses, up to which the Alde is navigable for vessels of 100 tons burthen. About 17,000 quarters of barley are shipped here yearly for London and other markets, by Mr. Newson Garrett, who has near the Bridge large warehouses, an extensive malting house etc.; the buildings on the south side being in the hamlet of Dunningworth, and parish of Tunstall.' (25)

Newson Garrett had begun his malting business at Snape in 1854 and built the Maltings there; although his home was in Aldeburgh a few miles away on the Suffolk coast, he tended to live at Snape during the period of winter malting.

Today Snape Maltings have been transformed into a crafts centre and renowned concert hall, famous for the Aldeburgh Festival and the music of Benjamin Britten and Peter Pears.

There was a short railway line to Snape, just a mile-and-a-half long and opened on the same day in 1859 as the other branch line to Framlingham, but it only ever carried goods and not passengers, so presumably the Coultas children would have gone on foot to Snape from Farnham along the lanes and across fields. They would probably have known the train drivers and waved to them as they passed, or chatted to them when they arrived at the station. Perhaps a highlight of the summer months was to go and join the crowds at the horse fair which was held every year at Snape Bridge on August 11th. It was also called Dunningworth Fair and continued to be a popular annual event until 1908. The children would be able to walk for miles under the wide Suffolk skies along the river banks or spend time watching the ships load and unload their cargoes. Standing beside Snape Maltings today, it is possible to imagine the fun they could have had playing games of hide and seek among the reeds on the marshes that stretch out from the bridge towards Iken and the sea.

Chapter Five

Change of Fortune

The family must have been thrilled when a second son, John Henry Coultas, was born towards the end of 1871, even though it meant another mouth to feed. By the following year however, their happy though hard-working lifestyle was destined to change for ever. Around April 1872, Eliza developed the dreaded disease of phthisis, and by January 15th 1873 she was dead. She was just forty years old and the children were still young – the eldest Mary Betsy was thirteen, Eliza Ann eleven, Susannah nine, Robert seven, Sarah Mabel just five, Louisa Charlotte three and baby John Henry only a little over a year old.

Life expectancy in mid-Victorian times was much shorter than it is today, and many adults did not survive beyond the age of forty. There were various reasons; for example, as Dr Lori Williamson says:

'A poor diet, which one initially would not equate with country life, weakened resistance to illness. Many country dwellers were self-sufficient and prepared nutritionally adequate meals from the produce of their garden or allotment...however,...not all country wives were resourceful when it came to feeding their families; nutrition was little understood, and country women in general found themselves criticised by their contemporaries for their inability to produce nourishing soups. Florence Nightingale censured these same women for refusing to believe in sanitation and for helping to spread disease by their lack of domestic skills and ignorance about hygiene. Bread, lard and tea, sometimes mixed with dust by unscrupulous village shop-owners to make it go further, formed the basis of the rural diet for women and children; as the principal wage-earners it was the men in a family who received what meat was available.' (1)

Illness and disease could also spread in rural areas in other ways:

'Many country men, women and children were adversely affected by...cramped, damp, poorly ventilated cottages which had neither drains nor privies but which were often in close proximity to open cesspits and filthy ditches....Even in areas which boasted privies, often no more than earth closets, there was still the problem of cleaning them out...Piles of human and animal excrement were breeding grounds for disease-carrying flies and water-borne germs, while the over-crowded conditions of many country cottages contributed to air-borne illnesses.' (2)

The phthisis from which Eliza Coultas died was a terrible disease – we would know it today as tuberculosis (TB) or consumption – which claimed many lives, particularly those of females. In Suffolk the situation was even worse than elsewhere. John Glyde junior, writing about the state of Suffolk in 1851, was in no doubt about that:

The mortality from phthisis or consumption is truly alarming. This disease is doubly and trebly more fatal than any other disease on the list, and the deaths of Suffolk females from this are far above the average of England, as well as of that of the neighbouring counties. In the four years ending 1842, there were 350 more deaths from consumption in Suffolk than in Essex, although the total deaths were 1,200 less than they were in Essex. Consumption is the great inexorable destroyer of men and women in the prime of life, and the most eminent of the medical profession have been baffled in their efforts to disarm it of its fatal powers.' (3)

W Somerset Maugham, in his book '*Of Human Bondage*', gives a graphic account of the symptoms of phthisis as he describes the plight of a young patient in the doctor's surgery:

'Sometimes there was a tragedy. Once a young woman brought her sister to be examined, a girl of eighteen, with delicate features and large blue eyes, fair hair that sparkled with gold when a ray of autumn sunshine touched it for a moment, and a skin of amazing beauty. The students' eyes went to her with little smiles. They did not often see a pretty girl in these dingy rooms. The elder woman gave the family history, father and mother had died of phthisis, a brother and a sister, these two were the only ones left. The girl had been coughing lately and losing weight. She took off her blouse and the skin of her neck was like milk. Dr. Tyrell examined her quietly, with his usual rapid method; he told two or three of his clerks to apply their stethoscopes to a place he indicated with his finger; and then she was allowed to dress. The sister was standing a little apart and she spoke to him in a low voice, so that the girl should not hear. Her voice trembled with fear.

"She hasn't got it, doctor, has she?"

"I'm afraid there's no doubt about it."

"She was the last one. When she goes I shan't have anybody."

She began to cry, while the doctor looked at her gravely; he thought she too had the type; she would not make old bones either. The girl turned round and saw her sister's tears. She understood what they meant. The colour fled from her lovely face and tears fell down her cheeks. The two stood for a minute or two, crying silently, and then the older, forgetting the indifferent crowd that watched them, went up to her, took her in her arms, and rocked her gently to and fro as if she were a baby.

When they were gone a student asked: "How long d'you think she'll last, sir?"

Dr Tyrell shrugged his shoulders.

"Her brother and sister died within three months of the first symptoms. She'll do the same. If they were rich one might do something. You can't tell these people to go to St Moritz. Nothing can be done for them." (4)

Tragically, this was the situation in the Coultas family too. There was no chance that Eliza could have gone abroad to get better, unlike my father's sister who was able to recuperate and recover successfully from TB in Switzerland in the 1930s.

No sooner had the Coultas children mourned the loss of their mother than their little brother John Henry was to die at Framlingham (presumably at home in Brick Lane) just a few months later. He had been suffering for a fortnight with pneumonia and also had convulsions, so possibly he was a sickly infant from birth. A Mary Folkard of Parham was present at his death. Parents and families in Victorian times had to prepare themselves for early deaths of children; as Dr Williamson observes:

'one in every ten country children would not survive to adulthood, yet infant mortality rates were considerably lower in country areas than in the city, where the national average stood at 151 per 1000 throughout the nineteenth century.' (5)

Judith Flanders, in 'The Victorian House', writes:

'...children's health had always been a concern. Mortality rates for the general population were high, but they were dropping none the less: from 21.8 deaths per 1000 in 1868 to 18.1 per cent in 1888, down to 14.8 in 1908. ...(It must be remembered that until this point the most likely time of death was not in old age, but in infancy; as late as 1899, more than 16 per cent of all children did not survive to their first birthday). A child born in the earlier part of the century would probably have watched at least one of its siblings die; a child born in the 1880s would have had fewer siblings, and would also have had less chance of seeing them die.' (6)

The older Coultas children in particular must have had to work hard to keep things going at home and to care for their father James and the younger ones. To add to their pain, James himself was already ill with phthisis and a few months later – on November 7th 1873 – he followed his wife Eliza and son John Henry to the grave. It was Mary Folkard who registered the death of John Henry on April 4th, so James may even then have been too ill to do it himself or perhaps he had no alternative but to struggle to work that day. Both Eliza and James were buried in Farnham churchyard (and presumably John Henry as well); Eliza on January 19th 1873 and James on November 12th. No headstones have so far been found.

The Victorians, certainly the middle classes, were obsessed with death and the etiquette of funerals and mourning. There were strict rules about how long a period of mourning should be for different members of the family, the form the coffin and the horse-drawn hearse should take, and what clothes and jewellery should be worn. It was obligatory to wear black for mourning or white in the case of the death of a child. For children the small coffin would usually be white and might be carried by school friends or brothers and sisters. For working-class families however, such requirements would be out of the question in most cases because of the expense; mother might borrow a black dress or dye an old one and father might wear a crape [black] armband, but otherwise they would have to grieve for their loved ones as best they could and get on with their daily routine of hard work to keep themselves alive.

Although illness and death at an early age were to be expected in the mid-1800s, for the Coultas children it must have been a dreadful shock to find themselves orphaned and lose their baby brother, all within the one year. Despite their young age the two eldest children, Mary Betsy and Eliza Ann, had no option but to go out to service during the time their parents were ill; they had certainly left home by the time their father died. Eliza Ann appears to have been employed as a servant somewhere in Suffolk, but Mary Betsy may have gone farther afield; no records exist of where either of them worked at this time. With both parents dead, the concern now was to find somewhere for the remaining four children to live. The children's only relatives in Suffolk were their aunt and uncle, Ann and Isaac Allcock, who had their own family to bring up, so it would have been virtually impossible for them to care properly for several more children in their cottage at Benhall. Other Coultas relatives were scattered throughout England – in Nottinghamshire and Derbyshire, Sheffield, Durham and Lincolnshire and possibly Lancashire – and had their own lives to lead.

In such dire circumstances, what was to become of Susannah and Robert, Sarah Mabel and Louisa Charlotte?

Chapter Six

Curate to the Rescue

Ann and Isaac must have agonised over what to do for the best for their orphaned nieces and nephew. How could they be cared for and at the same time receive some sort of reasonable education? There seems to have been hardly any money available; when James Coultas died, the house contained nothing *'but a few articles of cottage furniture which were sold to satisfy creditors.'* (1) Regrettably in the short term there was only one solution. Six days after James's death, the four youngest children had to be taken into the Plomesgate Union Workhouse at Wickham Market. It must have been a horrible ordeal, particularly as workhouses generally had a bad reputation. Clearly their aunt and uncle at Benhall wanted them to stay there no longer than absolutely necessary, so Ann Allcock sought advice at once from the curate of their local parish church, the Rev E A Watkins. This turned out to be the wisest possible choice.

The curate of Benhall, the Rev Edwin Arthur Watkins, was both a literate and an efficient man, and in one respect he was unique. Before coming to Benhall in Suffolk he had been sent by the Church Missionary Society (CMS) to Canada and became the first missionary ever to be stationed permanently to a remote island community on the east coast of James Bay. It was a Hudson's Bay Company (HBC) post, known to Europeans as Big River or Fort George.

The HBC had been granted a charter in 1670 by King Charles II, covering a huge territory: some 40 per cent of modern Canada. In return for settling and developing the colony, the HBC was given a monopoly on the region's natural resources. Trading posts at the mouths of rivers were established, and trade arranged with the local Cree tribe. By the eighteenth century the HBC dominated the fur trade in Canada and elsewhere and also established missions and schools under the management of the church. The HBC had missions at Red River (south of present day Winnipeg in Manitoba) and at Moose Factory (now in Ontario), where Rev Watkins fully expected that he would be based. Newly ordained, just married at the age of twenty five (2) and full of pioneering zeal, he and his wife Ann arrived there in the HBC vessel *Prince Albert* in 1852, to be met by Bishop David Anderson, the first bishop of an immense diocese known as Rupert's Land that had been created in 1849. Bishop David had journeyed a very considerable distance by canoe from diocesan headquarters at Red River for his first episcopal visit to James Bay. Edwin and Ann stayed at Moose Factory overnight, only to discover to their disappointment the following morning that the bishop had other plans for them. They were to be stationed about 200 miles farther north, on the northeast corner of James Bay, in the much more isolated community of Fort George. It was here that the Rev Watkins would become missionary to the Cree Indians from 1852 to 1857. One of the bishop's intentions was that Edwin would also extend Christianity to the Inuit people (until recently referred to as Eskimos) and the HBC's plans for commercial hunting of beluga whales at Great and Little Whale Rivers seemed to guarantee Fort George's importance as a mission. (3)

For the Rev Watkins, however, the posting lived up neither to his hopes nor his expectations. He found life at Fort George difficult and was often very frustrated. No doubt it was even harder, a real culture shock, for his young wife Ann, who had not had the benefit of her husband's years of missionary training. He did take trouble to learn the Cree language, taking lessons from Sarah, the wife of the HBC's chief trader, John Spencer. It was the Spencers who had first welcomed Edwin and Ann to the remote island on a rainy Sunday afternoon; John Spencer was *'exceedingly rejoiced to find that such a...respectable couple have been appointed to reside at this place, where their services will be a salvation to us poor creatures...'* Edwin was regarded as an accomplished preacher, at least by HBC employees in his Fort George congregation. John Spencer spoke of his:

'beautiful discourses', the *'wholesome lesson'* and *'the unmistakable pleasure of listening to the edifying sermons of that able preacher the Revd Mr Watkins.'* (4)

Edwin worked hard at translating or adapting prayers and parts of the Bible to make Christianity more accessible to the Cree. By October 1853 he had mastered their language sufficiently to deliver his first sermon without an interpreter. He would have learned *'Wat chia'* for 'welcome' or 'goodbye' (said to be derived from a British sailor's salutation 'what cheer'), *'Chin is kum din'* for 'thank you', *'Ituk'* for 'caribou' and *'Mistuk'* for 'tree'. The prayer book became the 'large book', a pencil or pen was a 'book-stick', the bishop was 'great praying chief' and England was 'across the water country.' The Bible, known as the 'great book', was not yet translated, and Edwin, writing in 1853, prayed that God would hasten the translation of the entire Bible, so that *'each wandering family might have a copy to guide their feet unto the way of peace.'* Probably his greatest achievement was in the field of translation; he compiled the first Cree Dictionary, with 6000 words, which was later revised and published by the General Synod of the Anglican Church. His wife Ann helped as best she could, assisting him with handwritten copies of the Lords Prayer and the Ten Commandments, and giving to eastern Cree women lessons in sewing English-style dresses, since many of them (unlike those at Moose Factory) still wore clothes made of caribou skin. Often it was the women who received religious instruction if they were not having to haul the caribou home, since the men were often hunting or haymaking at Fort George, or just lying about after the excitement of the chase and smoking their pipes. (5)

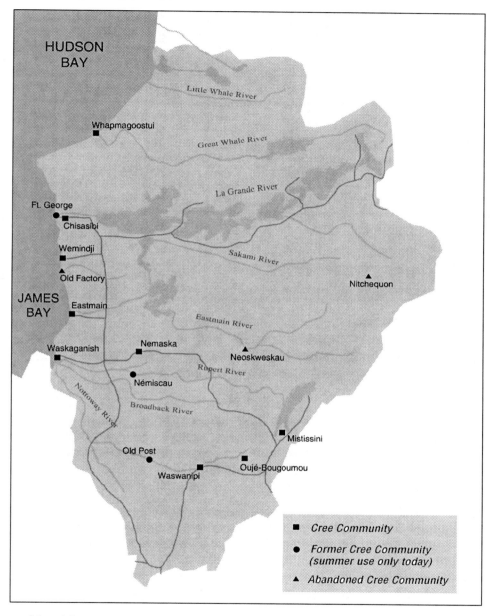

Map of Cree communities of Quebec, Canada, showing James Bay and Fort George where the Rev.
Watkins was based, with present-day Chisasibi.

Cree syllabary

		p [p]	t [t]	k [k]	c [ʧ, ts]	m [m]	n [n]	s [s]	š [ʃ]	y [j]	w [w]	r [r]	l [l]
ê [e:]	ᐁ	ᐯ	ᑌ	ᑫ	ᒉ	ᒣ	ᓀ	ᓭ	ᔐ	ᔦ	ᐍ	ᕃ	ᓓ
i [i]	ᐃ	ᐱ	ᑎ	ᑭ	ᒋ	ᒥ	ᓂ	ᓯ	ᔑ	ᔨ	ᐐ	ᕆ	ᓕ
î [i:]	ᐄ	ᐲ	ᑏ	ᑮ	ᒌ	ᒦ	ᓃ	ᓰ	ᔒ	ᔩ	ᐒ	ᕇ	ᓖ
o [o]	ᐅ	ᐳ	ᑐ	ᑯ	ᒍ	ᒧ	ᓄ	ᓱ	ᔓ	ᔪ	ᐔ	ᕈ	ᓗ
ô [o:]	ᐆ	ᐴ	ᑑ	ᑰ	ᒎ	ᒨ	ᓅ	ᓲ	ᔔ	ᔫ	ᐖ	ᕉ	ᓘ
a [a]	ᐊ	ᐸ	ᑕ	ᑲ	ᒐ	ᒪ	ᓇ	ᓴ	ᔕ	ᔭ	ᐙ	ᕋ	ᓚ
â [a:]	ᐋ	ᐹ	ᑖ	ᑳ	ᒑ	ᒫ	ᓈ	ᓵ	ᔖ	ᔮ	ᐛ	ᕌ	ᓛ
	ᐦ	ᑊ	ᐟ	ᐠ	ᐨ	ᒼ	ᐣ	ᐢ	ᐡ	ᐩ	ᐤ	ᕒ	ᓬ
	ᐦ	ᐸ	ᑕ	ᑲ	ᒐ	ᒪ	ᓇ	ᓴ	ᔕ	ᔭ	ᐤ	ᕋ	ᓚ
	h [h, ʔ]	p [p]	t [t]	k [k]	c [ʧ, ts]	m [m]	n [n]	s [s]	š [ʃ]	y [j]	w [w]	r [r]	l [l]

Sample text in Cree

ᒥᓯᐍ ᐃᓂᓂᐤ ᑎᐯᓂᒥᑎᓱᐏᓂᐠ ᐁᔑ ᓂᑕᐏᑭᐟ ᓀᐢᑕ ᐯᔭᑿᐣ ᑭᒋ ᐃᔑ ᑲᓇᐚᐸᒥᑯᐏᓯᐟ
ᑭᐢᑌᓂᒥᑎᓱᐏᓂᐠ ᓀᐢᑕ ᒥᓂᑯᐏᓯᐏᒪ᙮ ᐁ ᐸᑭᑎᒪᒪᒋᐠ ᑲᑫᔭᐌᓂᑕᒧᐏᓂᓂᐤ ᓀᐢᑕ
ᒥᑐᓀᓂᒋᑲᓂᓂᐤ ᓀᐢᑕ ᐏᒋᑵᓯᑐᐏᓂᐠ ᑭᒋ ᐃᔑ ᑲᒪᐚᐸᒥᑐᒋᐠ᙮

Transliteration

Misiwe ininiw tipenimitisowinik eshi nitawikit nesta peywakankici ishi kanawapamikiwisit kistenimitisowinik nesta minikowisiwima. e pakitimamacik kakeyawenitamowininiw nesta mitonenicikaniniw nesta wicikwesitowinik kici ishi kamawapamitocik.

Translation

All human beings are born free and equal in dignity and rights. They are endowed with reason and conscience and should act towards one another in a spirit of brotherhood. – *(Article 1 of the Universal Declaration of Human Rights)*

Cree Syllabics from Canada, showing the syllabary, with sample text and translation for Article 1 of the Universal Declaration of Human Rights. Edwin Watkins worked hard to master these syllabic characters (of which there are several modified versions), using them to communicate with the Cree Indians in the 1850s and to translate Christian texts.

As well as trying to master the Cree dialect, the Rev Watkins must have learnt some of the Inuit language; CMS archives relating to him refer to commandments, Lord's Prayer and a few verses of scripture in Eskimo in 1853. He is credited with being the person who first introduced the syllabic writing system (invented for the Cree and owing its origins to Pitman's Shorthand) to the Inuit in 1855 at Fort George and at Little Whale River, which was even farther north, beyond the tree line on Hudson Bay. In the same year he prepared a small book of gospel selections in Inuktitut syllabics and sent it to the Rev John Horden at Moose Factory (another missionary with translation and syllabic skills) who printed it on his mission press. It was one of the earliest items to be so printed and the only one in Inuktitut. Only one copy is known to have survived. On June 19th 1856 Watkins recorded:

This morning I spent an hour and a half with an Esquimaux youth, who had come…from Little Whale River…He seemed very anxious to acquire a knowledge of the syllabic characters.'

Nevertheless, Edwin often doubted that he was making any progress at all in bringing Christianity to the local people, whether it was the Cree, the Inuit or those who worked for the HBC. He felt in terms of learning they were always *'beginning & never making progress.'* Disillusioned and at times resentful, he wrote in 1853 *'Fort George is not nearly so important a field of missionary labour as I was given to understand.'* Some Christian concepts were difficult to teach and translate; as John S Long highlights as an example, 'feed my lambs' would have meant little to Indians who knew all about seals and whales but had never seen a sheep. In 1855 Watkins found the Cree Indians were *'so clouded by a host of superstitious notions that there seems but little prospect of success with the adult population.'* On the other hand he was able to report that the eight children attending his English-language day school were making steady and satisfactory progress,

'especially in Scripture knowledge in which I think they would…be found to equal most of the same age in England.' (6)

At least one happy event occurred while Edwin and Ann Watkins were at Fort George; their first child, Arthur, was born there in 1857 or 1858. Despite (or perhaps partly because of) this, Edwin was very keen to leave this remote island mission, where he certainly would not miss the *'indifferent sullenness and shameless ingratitude'* of Indians and HBC employees alike. The place was for him:

'a desolate portion of the Lord's vineyard' and so far distant from civilization that he was *'for all practical purposes…further removed from my nearest neighbour than persons in England are from the inhabitants of Calcutta.'*

Even his latest newspaper was at least eighteen months old. Initially therefore he must have been delighted to hear of his removal to Red River though he pleaded that he should *'not to be required to learn another language'* which he regarded as *'drudgery'.* (7) On his way back from James Bay he spent the winter of 1857–58 at Mapleton on Red River before moving to Cumberland House with the

Nepowewin mission (now Nipawin in Saskatchewan) from 1858 to 1860. He appears then to have moved again, this time to the Devon Mission founded at what became known as The Pas. (8) His family increased during this time; daughters Alice and Ellen were born at Devon in 1860 and 1862. Even then the situation did not improve; these new postings after leaving Fort George (which relocated to the mainland in 1980 and is known in Cree as *Chisasibi*, meaning 'Old' or 'Great' River) still failed to satisfy Edwin, although he seems to have stayed busy, translating the Gospel of St Luke in syllabic characters in 1859 and ordering supplies for Cumberland (1859 and 1860), Nepowewin (1858 and 1859) and Devon (1861). Yet he continued to be disheartened and finally left Canada with Ann and their young family to return to England in 1863. (9)

He may have spent a year or so of rest and reflection back in 'across the water country' after his mixed fortunes in Canada, but by November 26th 1864 he was ready to be licensed by John Thomas, bishop of the diocese of Norwich, to be the curate of Benhall in Suffolk at an annual salary, payable quarterly, of £80. He had been nominated to the position by the vicar of Benhall, the Rev Horace Mann Blakiston BD, and the licence made clear that the curate was to reside in the parish. He settled down to rural life in the county, which must have seemed appealing and greatly civilised compared with the world of the Cree and the Inuit; the 1871 Census shows Edwin aged forty-four and Ann aged forty-six living in the Rector's House at Benhall with their three children, Arthur aged fourteen, Alice (said to be ten but probably twelve) and Ellen aged ten. A young boarder, twelve year-old Ernest White, and two unmarried servants, housemaids Eliza Fiske aged twenty-one and Anna Ashley aged seventeen, both born in Suffolk, made up the rest of the household.

At Fort George, the Rev Watkins had experienced great disappointment when he could not affect the lives of the people as much as he would have wished. He was now a father himself. Perhaps these factors led him to feel compassion for the orphaned Coultas children and to understand something of their plight. In Suffolk at least, there was an opportunity for Edwin, in line with his duty as a clergyman to help the poor, to take positive action that could make a difference. He certainly wasted no time in putting pen to paper on behalf of his parishioner Ann Allcock and her nieces and nephew. There is no evidence that he consulted his vicar but this could have been because the Rev Blakiston was not very well. He had been granted licence by the bishop on April 17th 1871 to be absent from the benefice until May 31st 1872 '*on account of your ill health and incapacity of body*', and although he was back in action and signing off the churchwarden's accounts by April 1873, much of the practical work of the parish may have been left to his curate. Whatever the situation, Edwin Watkins took it upon himself to act swiftly and to seek for the Coultas children a more agreeable and permanent home.

*Scenes at modern-day Chisasibi, Canada (formerly Fort George). Rev Edwin Watkins found this remote area beside James Bay to be **"a desolate portion of the Lord's vineyard."** Today the region forms part of Northern Quebec.*

He already knew of the Christian work and teaching of a Mr George Müller, who had founded New Orphan Houses at Ashley Down Horfield in Gloucestershire – now part of Bristol. The curate was very impressed by Mr Müller's sermons and writings, and had tried to follow his philosophy in his own preaching from the pulpit. So when Ann Allcock asked him what could be done for the children, he thought immediately of sending them to the Müller Homes. Just eleven days after James Coultas's death, on November 18th, the Rev. Watkins wrote to George Müller in the following terms:

'Dear Sir

'As one of the cottagers in this Parish has asked me if I could do anything for some nephews and nieces of hers who have recently been deprived of both their parents by death, I have thought that perhaps you might be able to take one or two of these into your Orphan Houses. There are <u>seven</u> children but the two oldest are out at service. The other <u>five</u> (10), one boy and four girls, are now from necessity placed in the Workhouse of this Union – The mother died last January & the father, who was a Railway labourer, died on the 7th inst. – The <u>three requirements</u> which you make in the case of orphans are met in these children, but all particulars can be forwarded to you at a future date, in case you could kindly entertain the application.'

Edwin Watkins ended his letter with fulsome praise for the work of Mr Müller:

"I am thankful to find from recent notices of your labours in 'The Xtian' (sic) that our gracious God continues to support you & to entrust to you the means of doing so large an amount of good to the bodies & souls of so many of our fellow creatures. It may perhaps be some slight encouragement to know that I have several times referred to your labours when preaching to our villagers & have read to them extracts from your Reports at our Missionary Prayer Meetings, hoping thereby to encourage them to receive more <u>faith</u> & to abound more in <u>prayer.</u>

Praying that all grace may abound to you, believe me
Yours very faithfully
E A Watkins
(Curate of Benhall)' (11)

Chapter Seven

The Müller Homes

Who then was this Mr Müller and how did his orphan houses come about?

George Müller, founder of the New Orphan Homes, Ashley Down, Bristol. (1805-1898)

Born in Prussia in 1805, the son of a tax collector, George Müller led a rebellious and sinful life as a young man – stealing, lying, cheating and living the life of a playboy. He was supposed to be studying to be a Lutheran clergyman to please his father, but the law caught up with him and he ended up in prison. This immoral lifestyle was destined to come to an end, however, when he became a Christian at the age of twenty. One of his friends, a fellow student called Beta, told George of a prayer meeting which he often attended. George asked to go with him – and it was this meeting that changed his life. In 1829, having developed a passion for the Hebrew language, he made his way to London intending to train as a missionary to the Jews, but soon afterwards he became ill and almost died. Recuperating in Devon, he met Scotsman Henry Craik who was to become his closest friend. George accepted the pastorate of a church in Teignmouth, with an honorarium of £50, and began to learn much more about the scriptures and the preaching of God's word.

George married Mary Groves, and by 1832 Henry Craik had moved to Bristol and invited George and Mary to join him there. They did so, with Müller and Craik sharing a pastoral ministry at the Bethesda Chapel in Bristol. In 1834 George founded The Scriptural Knowledge Society (later to become the Scriptural Knowledge Institution or SKI). A worsening cholera epidemic and an ever-increasing number of homeless children at this time made him realise the need for immediate action, so in 1835 he called a public meeting with a view to opening an orphan home. He and Mary began, together with friends, to furnish a home in Wilson Street in the St Paul's area of Bristol to accommodate thirty girls, and this was followed by three further homes in the same street.

Mr Müller was convinced that God and the power of prayer would produce the necessary money to provide for the orphans without asking people for it. This somehow proved to be the case throughout his life; shortage of funds often meant that he had no idea where the next meal was coming from, yet someone always came forward with what was needed in cash or in kind. Roger Steer, in *'Delighted In God'*, illustrates the sort of problems that Müller overcame through faith in his work for the orphan children, especially in the early days:

'...the children neither knew of the difficulties nor lacked good food, clothes or warmth. But there were some narrow scrapes. At midday on Tuesday, February 8th 1842, there was enough food in all the houses for that day's meals, but no money to buy the usual stock of bread (for future use) or milk for the following morning; two houses needed coal. Müller thought that they had never been poorer and wrote that if God sent nothing before nine the next morning 'His name would be dishonoured.' Late in the afternoon nine plum cakes arrived, baked by order of a kindly lady. Encouraging – and no doubt tasty – as these were, the situation was still grim as Müller retired to bed that night...Next morning, [he] walked early to Wilson Street to discover how God would meet the need, only to find on arrival between seven and eight that it had already been met. A Christian businessman had walked about half a mile to his place of work when the thought occurred to him that Müller's children might be in need. He decided, however, not to retrace his steps then, but to take something to the homes that evening. But as he later told Müller: "I could not go any further and felt constrained to go back." He delivered three sovereigns to the boys' home. This gift, together with some other smaller sums, met the

needs for two days.' (1)

When the number of children in Wilson Street reached 130, it was clear that larger, purpose-built homes were needed. As Roger Steer indicates:

'Müller wanted the children to have more room to play. Also he wanted to be within easy reach of land which could be turned into gardens where the older boys could work. Another advantage of larger premises would be that all the laundry could be done at the Homes.' He was *'also concerned that the air at Wilson Street wasn't as bracing as it might have been and, bearing in mind that many of the children were unhealthy on arrival at the homes, he was anxious that they should be situated in as invigorating a position as possible. The teachers and staff, too, he thought, would be glad of somewhere where they could relax in a garden or walk in the fields after hours.'* (2).

After much prayer and consultation, he looked for a piece of land of six or seven acres on the outskirts of Bristol, and was able to purchase a very suitable site at Ashley Down for a reasonable price. The first home there, called Orphan House Number One and able to accommodate 300 children, opened in 1849 and George Müller recorded:

"Monday June 18th 1849 – great excitement at Wilson Street: the first children were ready to move up to Ashley Down. How the first sight of this large new building took their breath away! How they enjoyed the sound of the birds singing, the sight of cows grazing in the fields, and the view across the valley towards Stapleton! Once inside, even the fresh paint and newly polished woodwork smelt good, and the whole place was bright and well ventilated. By Thursday everyone, including the teachers and staff, had moved in: one hundred and forty people under one roof. By Saturday, there is already such a measure of order established in the house, by the help of God, as that things can be done by the minute hands of the time-pieces.' (3)

Increasing numbers of children led to further need to expand, with the result that Orphan House Number Two, which was immediately to the south of Home Number One and at right angles to it, opened in November 1857. It was larger than House Number One, with room for 400 girls: 200 infants and 200 girls aged eight and upwards. Müller was anxious to make sure the children were kept warm, so central heating was installed, which must have been a considerable luxury in those days.

Between 1834 and 1869 over £430,000 had been obtained for this important endeavour. By the time the Coultas children were being considered for entry into Mr Müller's care in the 1870s, he had bought even more land at Ashley Down and another three orphan houses had been built, with more than 2000 children being admitted. (4) This was pioneering work, begun some thirty years before the better-known Dr Barnardo started up his charity for poor orphan children in London's East End. The work grew and grew, both at the orphan houses and with SKI, which had by 1880 become responsible for seventy-two day schools with 7000 students in Bristol as well as in Italy, Spain and South America. Mary Müller gave great support to her husband and lived to see all five houses completed, spending nearly every day there until her death in 1870. George missed her greatly but two years later, following the marriage of his only surviving child Lydia to James Wright, he felt it was right to remarry. His new bride was Susannah Sanger whom he had known for twenty-five years.

The *'three requirements'* (5) for admission to the New Orphan Houses that the Rev Edwin Watkins referred to in his letter were not specified, but apparently Mr Müller did insist that all the children he cared for had lost both of their parents, that they were destitute and that the children had been born in wedlock. Unwed mothers and their illegitimate children were socially unacceptable at this time of strict Victorian values, and consequently George Müller and most similar charitable institutions were willing to accept only lawfully begotten orphans. Perhaps surprisingly, Mr Müller did not require that the children should come from a Christian background; often the children of non-Christians came to the orphan houses because of the high standard of care and education. The homes became well known throughout the country; even Charles Dickens, who in 1837 had highlighted the terrible plight of orphan children in his novel *'Oliver Twist'*, visited one day and toured the site in the company of two boys. Mr Dickens had not made an appointment and Mr Müller was too busy to take him round himself! Mr Dickens had *'heard a rumour that the children were badly treated and sometimes hungry'* (6) but during his visit he could find no fault. In fact he wrote a favourable account in the newspaper for which he was then working, with the result that many children were sent to Mr Müller from the London area and even farther afield.

The Ashley Down homes were regarded as the best thing in the country for orphan children of poor families and news of their standard of care quickly spread. Even as far away as the rural Suffolk village of Benhall, the Rev. Watkins was able to speak of Mr Müller's name being *'a household word with us'.* (7) It is of course possible that Edwin Watkins had come to hear of George Müller during his missionary days in Canada; one of the objectives of SKI as set out by Müller in 1834 had been *'to aid in supplying the wants of Missionaries and Missionary Schools'.* (8) He could also have heard about Müller's work and teachings from his old bishop, David Anderson, assuming they kept in touch, because not long after Rev Watkins had left Canada the bishop had resigned the see of Rupert's Land and become the incumbent of the parish church of Clifton in Bristol. He took a great interest in religious societies there, and would undoubtedly have known about SKI and the New Orphan Houses on Ashley Down.

The Rev Watkins' flattering words in his letter of November 18th seem to have had their desired effect. Within days, George Müller wrote back to say he could consider taking the Coultas children and preparations were begun to move some or all of them from the workhouse to the orphan houses at Bristol as quickly as possible. Just two days before Christmas 1873, the Curate sent various necessary certificates (9) and replies to questions to Mr Müller, saying:

'I hope the papers and answers to questions will be satisfactory, & I shall feel thankful if

you are able to take the four children or any of them.' He also asked *'if you would write to me instead of the Allcocks who reside in this Parish & I will see them after hearing from you.'*

This was *'to save time'* as he put it, though probably he doubted if the Allcocks were sufficiently literate to cope adequately with the necessary exchange of letters. Already the children had been given a 'Registered Number' for the homes – number 5092 – which Edwin Watkins usually added to his future correspondence by way of reference. (10)

By January he was able to confirm to Mr Müller that *'the boy'* [Robert Haythorne Coultas] *'is not under six years of age, and I am glad to say that one of his Uncles will soon take him from the Workhouse.'* (11) This meant that Robert would not have been accepted for admission to Ashley Down; Müller's philosophy from the beginning had been that the homes would be *'for truly destitute children and any orphan whose relatives are able and willing to pay for their maintenance will be ineligible.'* (12) Evidently Robert did in fact leave Suffolk almost at once to go and live in Lincolnshire with his Uncle George Coultas, who was a farmer at Langton by Wragby. (13) He seems to have been the most affluent member of the family, probably without children of his own. He may have felt bound to do something to help at least one of the orphans as he was now the head of the family, his father and two elder brothers all being dead before 1873. (14)

Robert's emotions as he coped with losing both parents and being sent to live with an uncle must have been similar to those of Philip Carey in W Somerset Maugham's book *'Of Human Bondage'* even though Philip came from a more middle-class background. Somerset Maugham knew personally what it was like to be orphaned at the age of ten, and he describes such an experience through the words of his hero Philip Carey, whose father had died suddenly some six months before:

'A woman servant came into a room in which a child was sleeping and drew the curtains…"Wake up, Philip" she said…"Your mother wants you"…She opened the door of a room on the floor below and took the child over to a bed in which a woman was lying. It was his mother. She stretched out her arms, and the child nestled by her side. He did not ask why he had been awakened. The woman kissed his eyes, and with thin, small hands felt the warm body through his white flannel nightgown. She pressed him closer to herself. "Are you sleepy, darling?" she said. Her voice was so weak that it seemed to come already from a great distance. The child did not answer, but smiled comfortably. He was very happy in the large, warm bed, with those soft arms about him…In a moment he closed his eyes and was fast asleep. The doctor came forwards and stood by the bedside.

"Oh, don't take him away yet", she moaned…Knowing she would not be able to keep the child much longer, the woman kissed him again;…she gave a sob. "What's the matter?" said the doctor. "You're tired."

She shook her head, unable to speak, and the tears rolled down her cheeks. "Let me take him." She was too weak to resist his wish, and she gave the child up. The doctor handed him back to his nurse…

It was a week later…The nurse bent down and kissed him, then began to shake out the cushions, and put them back in their places. 'Am I to come home?' he asked. 'Yes, I've come to fetch you'…It was in eighteen-eighty five…The question she had expected did not come, and so she could not give the answer she had prepared.

"Aren't you going to ask how your mother is?" she said at length.

"Oh, I forgot. How is mamma?"

Now she was ready. "Your mamma is quite well and happy."

"Oh, I am glad."

"Your mamma's gone away. You won't ever see her any more."

Philip did not know what she meant.

"Why not?"

"Your mamma's in heaven."

She began to cry, and Philip, though he did not quite understand, cried too…

…in a little while, she pulled herself together.

"Your Uncle William is waiting in to see you," she said…Emma [the nurse] *led Philip into the drawing room…"Here's Master Philip," said Emma. Mr Carey stood up slowly and shook hands with the little boy…"you're going to live with me now, Philip," said Mr Carey. "Shall you like that?"*

Two years before Philip had been sent down to stay at the vicarage after an attack of chicken-pox; but there remained with him a recollection of an attic and a large garden rather than that of his uncle and aunt.

"Yes."

"You must look upon me and your Aunt Louisa as your father and mother."

The child's mouth trembled a little, he reddened, but did not answer.

"Your dear mother left you in my charge."…Philip began to cry, and the nurse could not help crying too…Though Philip clung to her, she released herself gently. Mr Carey took the boy on his knee and put his arm round him.

"You mustn't cry," he said. "You're too old to have a nurse now. We must see about sending you to school."

"I want Emma to come with me,"…

"It costs too much money, Philip. Your father didn't leave very much, and I don't know what's become of it. You must look at every penny you spend."

As Emma was packing Philip's things for him to go and live with his Uncle and Aunt, he remembered that his Uncle said he might take something to remember his father and mother by. He decided on a little clock he had once heard his mother say she liked.

'With this he walked again rather disconsolately upstairs. Outside the door of his mother's bedroom he stopped and listened. Though no one had told him not to go in, he had a feeling that it would be wrong to do so; he was a little frightened, and his heart beat uncomfortably; but at the same time something impelled him to turn the handle. He turned it very gently, as if to prevent anyone within from hearing, and then slowly pushed the door open. He stood on the threshold for a moment before he had the courage to enter. He was not frightened now, but it

seemed strange…On the dressing-table were Mrs Carey's brushes and the hand mirror. In a little tray were hairpins…He had often been in the room when his mother was not in it, but now it seemed different…

Philip opened a large cupboard filled with dresses and, stepping in, took as many of them as he could in his arms and buried his face in them. They smelt of the scent his mother used…The strangeness of the room left it, and it seemed to him that his mother had just gone out for a walk. She would be in presently and would come upstairs to have nursery tea with him. And he seemed to feel her kiss on his lips.

It was not true that he would never see her again. It was not true simply because it was impossible. He climbed up on the bed and put his head on the pillow. He lay there quite still.

Philip parted from Emma with tears, but the journey to Blackstable amused him, and, when they arrived, he was resigned and cheerful.' (15)

No doubt once eight-year-old Robert arrived in Lincolnshire he would, though missing his sisters, have felt reasonably at home in another agricultural county. When not in school, he would most likely have been put to work by giving his uncle a helping hand around the fifty-acre farm.

Back in Suffolk, the Rev Watkins also made necessary arrangements for the names and addresses of the orphans' close relatives – their maternal grandparents, uncles and aunts living around the country – to be listed and sent to Mr Müller. (16) None of the relatives, except for Uncle George, appears to have offered to take one or more of the children to live with them; probably they had neither the space nor the money to feed three extra girls. Although the curate managed to obtain the required information, it was at the expense of his usual neatness and efficiency. His letter to Ashley Down, addressed to a Mr Daniel French on January 22nd 1874, contained an apology, albeit a somewhat condescending one:

'I beg to return the paper which you sent me for signatures some little time ago. It is a good deal messed and dirtied, having been sent to several different places & to a class of persons who are not much accustomed to the use of pen & ink.' (17)

The actual paper looks rather more literate than Edwin Watkins made out, however, and considering it had been all over the country it appears to be in reasonably good condition.

Rev Watkins was careful to make it very clear that while he had made the application for admission of the children as curate of the parish *'in which one of the aunts lives',* (18) he did not undertake any personal responsibility should the children be dismissed from Ashley Down. That would be entirely a matter for the named relatives and not for him. Although relatives of the children seeking admission to the orphan houses were required to give an undertaking to take them back if absolutely necessary, Mr Müller was in fact very reluctant for this to happen. Roger Steer writes:

Just occasionally Müller had to expel a child who had become an unacceptably bad influence on the other children. But expulsion – that is, returning a child to a relative or guardian – was always a last resort after repeated warnings and attempts to reform the child; and after an offender had left, Müller and his staff followed him (or her) with their prayers.' (19)

Chapter Eight

A Setback

Susannah, Sarah Mabel and Louisa Charlotte Coultas were expected to depart for the orphan houses in Bristol in a matter of weeks, but unfortunately there was an unexpected delay. They began to suffer from ringworm, a skin disease that frequently affected the scalp in childhood, which meant that they were unable to leave Wickham Market until they were pronounced fully fit. Life must have seemed very grim indeed: their parents and baby brother recently dead, having to leave the cottage where they had been growing up and probably the school where all their friends were, their elder sisters away in service, and their surviving brother sent many miles away to Lincolnshire. On top of all this, they must cope with illness and adapt to life with all manner of people in the workhouse.

Wickham Market is a small town a few miles to the south of the villages where the Coultas and Allcock families lived. The Plomesgate Union Work House, near to the church and the market square, was completed in 1836/37 at a cost of around £7000, to serve forty-one parishes with some 21,000 inhabitants. Built in the Elizabethan style, it had room for around 370 inmates, with a boardroom and a chapel, kitchens and laundry blocks, and staff accommodation including a separate Master's House. The weekly cost of maintaining inmates in 1844 was 1s 10¾d for food and 7d for clothing. (1) The inmates were divided into men, women, boys and girls, with each category having a dormitory, a dining room, a day room and a small courtyard surrounded by high walls. A single story extension for old people was added later as well as a pest house for infectious cases. Two new sick wards were built, detached from the main building itself, in 1845, and from the 1850s there were two if not three nurses to look after those who were ill. (2)

The board of guardians (for the poor), with representatives for each of the parishes who were elected annually, met weekly on the premises. The chairman of the board when the Coultas orphans were first sent there was a Mr James Pettit, but on April 20th 1874 there was an election for a new chairman, with John George Sheppard Esq being elected by a very slender majority – thirteen votes out of twenty-five present. True to form, Frederick Snowden Corrance of Parham was one of ten *ex officio* guardians appointed in addition to the forty-three board members elected each year.

Deben Court, Wickham Market, formerly the Plomesgate Union Workhouse.

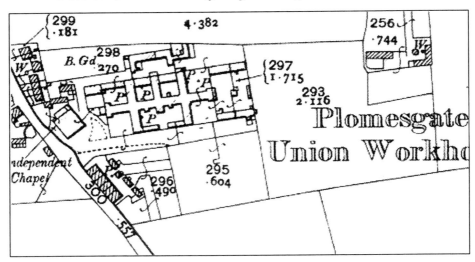

The guardians with their new chairman decided to set up several committees – a house committee (for matters concerning the workhouse), a finance & supply committee, an assessment committee and a vaccination committee – and agreed to meet fortnightly rather than weekly between June and October. This would allow the farmers on the board extra time to attend to their crops and harvesting in the summer months. In fact a majority of board members were farmers, who, says E P Cockburn,

'were the main employers in (this rural) area and therefore interested to keep wages low and the poor rate under control.' (3)

The guardians were often preoccupied with gathering in the levy on each parish for poor relief including maintenance of parishioners in the workhouse. All parishes were expected to contribute but there were many struggles to collect the levies and to get the relatives of the paupers to pay their share. The guardians also dealt with 'Out Relief' to help poor parishioners in need in their own homes – there were 736 in March 1874.

The workhouse master at this time was a Mr George Mason, who earned a salary of about £100 a year with accommodation and keep. He and his wife were there for an impressive forty-two years from 1854 to 1896. There were around 120–130 paupers at any one time, though numbers inevitably varied. In 1851 the total number was 103, including eleven sick and elderly, eighteen orphans or deserted children, thirty-eight single adults and a few women with children. (4) For maintenance of Susannah, Sarah and Louisa Coultas from November 13th to December 12th 1873, thirty days each, the guardians of the Plomesgate Union required the sum of £1, 17 shillings and 6 pence. Perhaps the children's aunt Ann had to pay this or at least part of it; the only record of money being paid into James Coultas's estate was 4 shillings and 6 pence on November 29th 1873 by way of medical order and relief. This payment came from Mr Ellis S Gleed, the relieving officer of the Plomesgate Union. (5)

The chief officials at the workhouse were the master and matron, the school master and school mistress, the porter who was responsible for keeping order, the medical officer and the chaplain. The chaplain was often but not always the vicar of Wickham Market, who would visit regularly and take a service on Sundays. The medical officers were all Wickham Market doctors and like the chaplain, non-resident. Again, they gave many long years of service; Dr George Keer, who attended to the Coultas children when they were unwell, was medical officer for forty-three years from 1853 to 1896.

The girls would have been expected to wear uniform and, provided they were well enough, would have received some education. Under an Act of 1834, Unions were by law required to provide at least three hours of schooling each day for workhouse children. At Wickham Market a nursery was provided for children over eighteen months and under school age, while a school master or mistress looked after school age children and shared their supervision with the master and matron. The Coultas girls should certainly have been taught reading, writing and arithmetic, with doubtless some religious instruction as well. The school master at the time was Mr Alfred Dorling while the school mistress, who would have taught the Coultas girls, was Miss Charlotte W Turtill. Then, as so often the case today, the man was paid more than the woman; Alfred's quarterly salary was £7, 10s. 0d, whereas Charlotte's pay for the same period was only £6, 5s. 0d. Perhaps this was one factor that persuaded her that it was time to move on; during the time that Susannah, Sarah Mabel and Louisa Charlotte were at Wickham Market, Charlotte Turtill asked the board for a testimonial as she had applied for a new appointment at the parish school at Syleham in the north of the county near the Norfolk–Suffolk border. She had been teaching at the workhouse since March 1870 and must have been successful in securing the new post, as the guardians were advertising for another school mistress before the end of the year. The salary they were offering was £25 a year, with furnished apartments, rations and washing provided in the workhouse.

After advertisements in the *Ipswich Journal, Suffolk Chronicle* and the *Local Government Chronicle,* seven ladies applied for the teaching post and three were short-listed although only two went for interview. Up to forty shillings was available to the candidates for travelling expenses, and the one elected would be required (like Pamela Rackham at Parham School) to pass an examination for a certificate by Her Majesty's Inspector of Schools at his next visit. One of the two interviewed was a Miss Lucretia Turtill, aged twenty-one, of Wickham Market (Charlotte Turtill's sister in fact) but on this occasion she was unsuccessful (6) and the appointment went, by unanimous decision of the guardians, to twenty-year-old Miss Catherine Green of Flowton, near Ipswich. She was to take up her post on January 25th 1875. Books of the school masters, school mistress, chaplain and porters were regularly examined by the guardians and signed by the chairman of the board, so the new young school mistress would certainly be kept on her toes. Perhaps this was just as well, for the staff did not always do as they should. In 1876, the minutes of the board of guardians state that

The master complained that the school master had several times been out all night, or been out late and the porter had locked him out and not told the master. The porter was dismissed because there was no one on duty to look after the children at night.'

This would suggest that the master was prepared to supervise in the absence of the school master. (7)

As E P Cockburn records, diet at the workhouse was laid down in great detail by the Poor Law commissioners and any variation had to be authorised. The 'Dietary' for 1842 (not much changed by 1883) showed the following for the men:

Dinner:	1 day	8 oz meat; ¾ lb vegetable
	1 day	5 oz bacon; ¾ lb vegetable
	1 day	1½ pints soup; 8 oz bread
	4 days	2 oz cheese; 8oz bread
Supper:	every day	1½ oz cheese; 7 oz bread

Women had basically the same, but one or two ounces less of bread, bacon and meat. Children under nine, like Sarah Mabel Coultas and her sister Louisa Charlotte, were *'dieted with such food as the guardians shall direct'*, while children aged 9–13 including Susannah would have had the same as the adult women.

Those who were sick were given diets according to the direction of the medical officer. For example, the convalescent diet, which the girls may have had while they were recovering from ringworm, consisted of:

Breakfast: Gruel (sweet porridge with treacle added) or
water porridge
Dinner: Broth and bread
Supper: Bread, butter, tea

Every patient, whatever their diet, had three-quarters of a pound of bread and an ounce of butter daily. These diets sound quite harsh by modern standards, but the inmates may well have fared better than the agricultural labourers and their families outside, except that their menus were probably not quite so rigid or monotonous.

Supplies for the inmates and resident staff were controlled by the board, with quarterly contracts being invited and suppliers and prices agreed. The main items purchased were bread, flour, cheese, meat, potatoes, butter, sugar, oatmeal and porter. Other items were wood, coal, blankets, rugs, sheeting, hose, stays, calico, bed sacking, serge, worsted and blue check. Port wine, gin, whisky and brandy also appeared fairly regularly, presumably for the staff!

Workhouse discipline was fairly tight, and the normal punishment for 'misconduct' or 'disobedience' was to be locked up for three hours or so. Fortunately an 1837 Regulation prevented children in the Workhouse from being punished by any reduction in their diet. (8)

Some of the children (such as the three Coultas girls) were only temporarily in the workhouse but many had no other home. Efforts were made therefore to find live-in jobs for school leavers and even younger children too. The majority went into service; in 1841 the guardians had decreed *'a quarterly list of children aged 10–16 fit for service to be put on all Church doors of the Union.'* (9) It is not known how Mary Betsy Coultas and her sister, eleven-year-old Eliza Ann, obtained their positions in service but perhaps too that was through contacts at the local church. Other good ways to find a new servant, according to Judith Flanders in *'The Victorian House'*, were *'through the grapevine – via a friend, another servant, or the local tradesmen, who often acted as a clearing agency; by going to a registry office; by advertising or answering an advertisement.'* (10)

An inspector from the Poor Law Commission (later the Poor Law Board and then the Local Government Board) seems to have visited the workhouse frequently and on an informal basis. Within the regulations, efforts were made to help the children; for example, in 1843 orphans were given leave of absence to visit friends for a fortnight, and children were able to go to relatives for a holiday. In later years there are reports of boys being given permission to bathe in the river and of day trips to Yarmouth for the girls. (11) Perhaps the Coultas children were allowed out for the occasional visit to see aunt Ann and uncle Isaac and their sister Eliza Ann, or to meet up with old school friends, provided, presumably, that they were free from infection.

Plans were still going ahead for the Coultas girls to move to Bristol in the near future. On March 2nd 1874 the minutes of the weekly meeting of the guardians record that they *'directed the Clerk to sign the Authority on behalf of the Board to receive back the three children named Susannah Coultas, Sarah Mabel Coultas and Louisa Coultas should they be dismissed from the New Orphan Houses on Ashley Down commonly known as Mullers Asylum to which place it is proposed to send them.'* (12)

Distressingly however, the ringworm did not clear up quickly. One of the girls was fully recovered by April, but the infection was slow to leave the other two. The Rev Watkins went to see the relieving officer, who stated that *'the children Coultas do not seem to be much better.'*

Letter written by Rev Edwin Arthur Watkins to Mr I Prosser at the New Orphan Homes, Ashley Down, Bristol on 17th April 1874. The Coultas children were still not well enough to be moved from Suffolk, but he remains hopeful that the situation will soon change.

Aunt Ann Allcock then visited her nieces towards the end of April and spoke with the surgeon, but had to report back to the curate that they were not yet well enough to be moved. It was thought that in about a fortnight they might be fully fit, but this proved to be far too optimistic. (13) Once again the children were to feature in the minutes of the meeting of the board of guardians, on May 18th 1874:

"Ordered the Clerk write the Rev E A Watkins of Benhall to say the three children named Coultas were on Monday last reported by the Medical Officer as Cured of the

Ringworm – and were removed from the Sick Ward to the Girls School Room but since that time the disease has again made its appearance on one of the children who has again returned to the Sick Ward but as soon as they are reported by the Medical Officer to be cured the Guardians will inform him of the same.' (14) A letter to this effect was apparently sent to the Rev Watkins before the guardians met again the following week. (15)

The enforced delay and uncertainty led the curate to feel that he had no option but to write again, this time to Mr Prosser at the orphan houses in Bristol, to say:

'I think it would be unfair to other poor orphans for the vacancies to be kept open, and no doubt there are numerous applications. At any rate the matter must be left <u>entirely</u> with Mr Müller & if he think proper to fill up the vacancies so let it be. I regret very much that there has been this unexpected delay.' (16)

There were indeed many applications for orphans to be admitted into the Müller Homes; in the 1860s there was a waiting list of nearly 1,000 children, and no doubt there was a similar situation at the time Mr Watkins was writing on behalf of the Coultas girls. This latest letter also coincided with a difficult and anxious time for George Müller personally, as his second wife Susannah had developed typhoid and was seriously ill between March and May of 1874. Thankfully by September she was fit enough to travel to the Isle of Wight where she made a full recovery, but this was probably the reason why Mr Prosser and other members of staff (Müller called them his 'fellow labourers') were corresponding with Edwin Watkins at this time rather than Mr Müller himself.

In the event, the children's ringworm persisted and it turned out to be several more months before the surgeon could pronounce them fit enough to be removed from Wickham Market.

Chapter Nine

New Beginnings

Eventually, on October 31ˢᵗ the Rev Watkins – dedicated as ever, even though he was away either on holiday or business at Great Yarmouth at the time – was able to write and confirm to Mr Müller that the children were now *'quite recovered from Ringworm'*, and ask whether they could at last be received into Ashley Down. If so, he wanted to know *'what arrangement you make as to any particular day of the week or hour of the day at which they can be admitted.'* (1) The reply is not known, but from the curate's response it seems the Müller Homes hoped the girls would arrive by early afternoon. On November 12ᵗʰ Edwin Watkins wrote again as follows, emphasising important issues with his customary underlining of words:

> *'Dear Sir*
>
> *I thank you for your letter giving an order for admission of the three children 'Coultas' into the Orphan House. Since receiving it I have seen the Aunt of the children and communicated its contents to her.*
>
> *As the distance is great I am not sure that the children will be able to reach the House by ½ past 2 in the afternoon without sleeping one night on the way which will add to the expense, but if your rules do not allow of a little <u>liberty as to time</u> this must of course be done. Will you please send me word <u>if the rule must be strictly observed,</u> but if an hour or so can be allowed for travelling I will not trouble you to write.*
>
> *The children <u>have</u> suffered for a long time from ringworm or some skin affliction of that nature but are now certified to be perfectly free from it.*
>
> *With many thanks for your kindness, believe me, yrs faithfully*
>
> *E A Watkins'* (2)

On November 19th 1874, a full year after the death of their father, Susannah, Sarah Mabel and Louisa Charlotte were at last able to leave for Ashley Down. Aunt Ann went with them on the journey from Suffolk, but the records do not show if they succeeded in arriving by 2.30 pm or whether they had to stay somewhere overnight. Nor is it known how they travelled, but more than likely it would have been by train, possibly for free, since their father and uncle were both railway employees. It would certainly have been a long, tiring and anxious journey. If they journeyed by train they would have taken the Great Western Railway (affectionately called 'God's Wonderful Railway') and arrived at the very imposing Bristol Station, designed by Isambard Kingdom Brunel in 1841 and extended in the 1870s. The children would have found this station, the oldest railway terminus in the world, enormously grand by comparison with those at Parham and Framlingham and rather forbidding. Another train – on the Bristol and South Wales Line – would take them to Ashley Hill Station, which stood close to what was to become their new home.

George Müller's Five Orphan Houses. The Coultas girls were in House Number Two.

Müller's New Orphan House Number One (opposite House Number Two) in 2004. Both these houses now form part of the City of Bristol College.

The children must have been apprehensive as to what to expect. They would surely have missed Mary Betsy, Eliza Ann and Robert Haythorne, as well as aunt Ann and uncle Isaac and the cousins they were leaving behind in Benhall. It can't have been easy for Ann Allcock either, having to make the long journey back to Suffolk on her own after leaving the girls at Ashley Down. Susannah, being the eldest of the three, was received into the girls' department of New Orphan House Number Two, while her younger sisters went into the Infant Department of the same house.

House Number Two was just a stone's throw away from House Number One, which Roger Steer describes as follows:

'...*over 300 people sat down every day to meals on Ashley Down including a staff of over thirty. Every Wednesday afternoon parties of visitors were shown around...*"We met at the door" *one visitor recalled,* "a little after two o'clock...When the doors were opened, we found ourselves in a very small hall, from whence a stone staircase leads up into a spacious room in the central building, where the visitors wait for their guide. This room is a perfect square, with the four angles taken off by the width of the windows, which we found looked into large pitched play-courts, with covered sheds for the children's use in wet weather. One court we saw was appropriated to infants of both sexes, a number of whom were toddling about under the charge of two or three older girls; another to girls; the third to boys; while the fourth window overlooks the part of the garden through which visitors approach.*

'...*We proceeded into the Infants' Day Room, where we found a tribe of little things, under the care of the nurse. Ranged round one side of this room are a number of little basket beds, for the use of the youngsters when tired of play...We found in one room about a dozen boys, under the care of a female, quietly and busily engaged in the very necessary employment of darning stockings...we admire the practical wisdom that insists, even in mending stockings, on teaching the best way. In the younger department are pigeon-holed cupboards for putting away their toys, when out of use. They were well furnished with nearly every description that a general shop would supply.*

'*The washing places, we observed, are furnished with baths, and on the walls is hung each child's little bag, numbered, with comb and hair-brush. The most scrupulous care is evidently bestowed to ensure thorough cleanliness of both persons and linen, as well as to guard against the communication of any infantile juvenile complaints from personal contact.*

'*In going through this most interesting establishment we were most forcibly impressed with the entire absence of a pauperised look in the dress and appearance of the children. The hair of the girls is kept beautifully neat, such as we could fancy a mother's love attended to; and there was a cheerful looking-up at the visitors, and a heart-smile on the young faces, which prove...that the presiding and pervading spirit which rules the entire establishment is the Law of Kindness.'* (3)

Similar arrangements and atmosphere no doubt existed at House Number Two even though it was bigger. Soon after their arrival Susannah, Sarah Mabel

71

and Louisa Charlotte would probably have met Mr Müller himself in his study, sitting at his plain wooden desk with his annotated Bible open beside him. They may have been in awe of this great man to begin with, but would doubtless have come to respect him and look on him as something of a father figure. According to Arthur Tappan Pierson, an American Bible teacher who knew Müller well:

'His form was tall and slim, always neatly attired, and very erect, and his step firm and strong. His countenance, in repose, might have been thought stern, but for the smile which so habitually lit up his eyes and played over his features that it left its impress on the lines of his face. His manner was one of simple courtesy and unstudied dignity: there was about him a certain indescribable air of authority and majesty…and yet there was mingled with all this a simplicity so childlike that even children felt themselves at home with him. In his speech, he never quite lost that peculiar foreign quality known as accent, and he always spoke with slow and measured articulation…He relished a joke that was free of all taint of uncleanness and that had about it no sting for others.' (4)

Although their world had been turned upside down by the death of their parents and they must have felt lonely and far from home at times, the Coultas girls seem to have settled well at Ashley Down, where they were able to receive a good education and preparation for life outside when they were old enough. George Müller's primary objective in founding the homes had not in fact been the welfare of the children, but rather that God should be seen to have provided all the needs of these boys and girls as a result of prayer and faith, without anyone being asked or approached. Nevertheless, the outcome was that most of the children prospered while at the New Orphan Houses, and were generally better off there than outside where diseases such as cholera and smallpox and poor sanitary conditions were rife. (5) It did not suit every child of course, but on the whole the orphans did well and were very grateful for the care and teaching that they received.

All children at the Müller Homes were smartly dressed. Susannah, Sarah Mabel and Louisa Charlotte would each have worn a navy cotton dress with white dots, protected by a green plaid cloak, shawl or white tippet depending on the weather. The girls also wore straw-coloured bonnets tied with an attractive band. In the words of Nancy Garton, quoted by Roger Steer:

'Indoors, girls up to the age of fourteen wore blue-checked gingham pinafores, cut high to the neck and with buttoning behind. Girls over fourteen who had left the schoolroom and were then called "House Girls" wore aprons with strings to distinguish them from their juniors. The most senior girls, those who were due to leave the Homes for situations within a few months, were known as "Cap Girls" and wore white caps, aprons to the waist and white collars. Every girl had five dresses. The stockings were all hand knitted by the girls; black wool for winter, and white cotton for summer…The shoes were mostly of the ankle strap variety.' (6)

Management of the girls' hair was clearly a matter of importance and pride, as Nancy Garton describes:

'The tiny girls had theirs almost as short as a boy's, but beautifully glossy and well brushed.

Those from about eight years old up to eleven had a Dutch bob, with centre parting and fringe, such as they could comb into place themselves without assistance. The older girls, who were capable of doing their own hair, were allowed to grow it to shoulder length or longer, and hold it back with a velvet ribbon band. The most senior girls put their hair up.' (7)

There were large numbers of staff: these included a school inspector, matrons, teachers, medical officers, nurses and Mr Müller's personal assistants. (8) The day started at 6 am for the orphans but this was not at all unusual in Victorian times. There was strict discipline but it was not a harsh regime. Food was wholesome and regular, with porridge every morning for breakfast and meat for dinner three times a week. There was plenty of fresh fruit and eggs, with milk and water to drink. On his or her birthday, each child could look forward to two eggs, one for themselves and one for their best friend. (9) This certainly sounds more varied than the monotonous diet experienced at Wickham Market. The children slept in dormitories, but with the beds, and cots for the younger ones, neatly made and well spread out in long light rooms with wooden floors.

Education was of a high standard, in a variety of subjects. In fact, George Müller often faced criticism that it was *too* high and 'above the station' of most of the children. He did not agree; on the contrary, he employed a school inspector to maintain the high standards he had set. In 1885, the year that Sarah Mabel Coultas was to leave Ashley Down, the average percentage of all children in their annual examination based on six subjects was 91.1 per cent. As Roger Steer records for that year:

The Annual Examination of the children was held during the months of February and March...The children were examined and arranged in the second, third, fourth, fifth and sixth standards in many particulars according to the Government Code. Each child was examined separately in reading. Each child showed his or her copy-book to determine the mark for writing. Ten questions were put on each of the following subjects, viz, on Scripture, Geography, History and Grammar. Six sums were given in Arithmetic. The answers were given on paper.' (10)

Life at Ashley Down was not all devoted to study for examinations. Healthy exercises and dressing up to give displays to visitors were encouraged. The children developed their sewing and embroidery skills; many of the samplers completed by the girls are exquisite, often in red thread, and much sought after in auction houses even today. They learned singing, composition and domestic science. There was practical work; for example, the boys would go on errands and spend time planting and weeding in the gardens. Throughout the year there would be daily worship and prayers and the children were also taken on Sundays to church or chapel. Every Good Friday all the children from the five homes who were old enough went on foot, in crocodile fashion, to Bethesda Chapel – a considerable distance – to hear George Müller preach.

The children were often taken out for walks, though at first the Coultas girls must have found the hills of Bristol hard going after the relatively flat countryside of Suffolk. In particular, the annual outing to Purdown, a field within walking distance from the orphanage, was a very popular treat:

'the children set off in the morning armed with either a pink or blue cotton bag filled with sweets and sweet biscuits to eat on the journey...on arrival at the field, the children of the five houses could mix as they pleased. The picnic lunch (of bread and cheese) and tea (bread, butter and cake) was transported to Purdown in large hampers...The outing ended with the launching of five fire balloons, one for each House.' (11)

Müller girls enjoying their annual outing to Purdown, all smartly dressed and wearing tippets and bonnets.

On special occasions, such as Mr Müller's birthday on September 27th, the children were given cake and enormous apple dumplings.

Christmas was another special time, with its trees and decorations, presents, carols, games and parties. Mr Müller wrote in his journal for December 23rd 1878, while the three Coultas children were in House Number Two:

'From Clifton we received for the children a number of dolls, some fancy boxes, albums, games, balls, tops and a great variety of other play-things – From Durdham Down, as Christmas presents for the orphans, dressed dolls, boxes and packets of chocolates and sweets, some drums, tops, balls, marbles, whips and guns, boxes of toys, books, fancy cards, paint boxers, transparent slates, pocket-handkerchiefs, wool ties and ruffs, baskets and boxes, pencils, trumpets and other play-things...From a Bristol wholesale house, fifteen boxes of fruit, ten boxes of oranges, ten boxes of figs, and a sack of nuts for the orphan's Christmas Treat.' (12)

As Roger Steer points out,

'Müller's large homes did offer some advantages which smaller ones cannot. Life may have been regimented, and the routine predictable, but the shared fun of so many youngsters living and growing up together meant that it was often jolly. There was also a stability and security about them which were absent from smaller homes.'

For example, in one small orphan home in London, members of staff were constantly changing, whereas teachers at Ashley Down would often stay there for many years. (13)

During the years that Susannah and her sisters were there, Mr and Mrs Müller were often away overseas. With the five New Orphan Houses well established, and in his seventieth year, George decided to embark on a preaching mission that was to last nearly seventeen years and include Europe, China, India, America and Australia. Whenever he and his wife returned they were always sure of a very warm reception. On July 8th 1878 for example, after a year's demanding tour of the United States which included an invitation to the White House, Mr Müller was to record:

'upon arriving in an open carriage at the top of Ashley Hill at half-past four, found a little army of boys and girls with almost all our helpers at the Orphan-Houses waiting to receive us. There, as we slowly drove along, the boys cheered heartily, and the girls waved their handkerchiefs, determined (as a by-stander remarked) to give us 'a right royal welcome'; and at the entrance of New Orphan House Number Three, a crowd of children closed around us, with loving, friendly greetings.' (14)

Perhaps Susannah Coultas and her sisters from House Number Two were part of that 'little army', waving their handkerchiefs along with all the rest.

Even as Susannah, Sarah Mabel and Louisa Charlotte were making progress with their studies at the Müller Homes, they were to receive another blow. News was to reach them that their older sister Eliza Ann had died in Suffolk on February 5th 1876 at the age of 14. Her death certificate shows that she too was a victim of the dreaded phthisis pulmonalis *(sic)* having suffered from it for nine months. Like her parents before her, she must increasingly have suffered from fatigue, shortness of breath and loss of appetite. In all probability she would have developed a hacking cough and fever, with perhaps swelling of her feet as her circulation began to fail. It must have been an agonising end to a young life. Her aunt (described on the certificate as Annie Alcock *(sic)* of Benhall) was present when Eliza Ann died at Benhall and was responsible for registering the death. Presumably Ann and Isaac had taken Eliza out of service and into their own home to care for her when she became too ill to work. Like her parents, Eliza was buried in the churchyard at Farnham.

Two years later, on April 22nd 1878, James' and Eliza's son Robert Haythorne was dead as well. Despite an open air life on the farm in Lincolnshire, he had suffered for two years from the same disease which had already been responsible for the deaths of three members of his family. His uncle George Coultas was present when he died at Langton – he was just twelve years old. He must have been attending the village Sunday School, because they remembered him with affection. A small book with a blue cover in my possession called *'Marian and her Cousins'* is inscribed on the fly leaf with the words *'In memory of Robert Coultas Langton Sunday School 1878.'* It was usual for most Victorian working class children, no fewer than 75.4 per cent in 1851, to have a Sunday School education, where they were encouraged to read the Bible and learn passages of scripture. Although published by the Society for the Propagation of Christian Knowledge (SPCK) in the 1870s, *'Marian and her Cousins'* was not a religious publication but a gentle, morality tale of a doctor's daughter brought up in London who hated the idea of spending a holiday with her country cousins George and Phil. Despite her misgivings, Marian came to love the rural life – and her initially despised cousins – during her visit, having learned much about a variety of birds, toads and mice, hedgehogs and bats, cattle and haymaking. The moral: it is wiser not to jump to conclusions until you are sure of the facts. A pencil note above the inscription in Robert's memory reads *'S M Coultas June 17th 1888'*, so presumably this little book was one of Sarah Mabel's treasured possessions, which has been passed on through the generations.

Illustrations from "Marian and her Cousins", published by the SPCK, and inscribed in memory of Robert Haythorne Coultas, Langton Sunday School, 1878. Despite misgivings, Marian learns to appreciate the delights of rural life and the company of her country cousins.

The children's aunt, Ann Allcock, did not survive for very much longer. She died at Benhall in November 1880 aged fifty-one, and soon afterwards her husband Isaac left the village. By the time of the 1881 Census he had changed his career, moving away from the railways to become a beer retailer at Cranford

Lane Beer House, Heston, Middlesex. His twenty-two year old daughter Alice, still unmarried, lived with him as his housekeeper, while eldest son Robert, by then aged thirty-one and married to Rosetta (*nee* Rice), was also a beer seller and living at The Beer House, 16 Tower Street, Southwark. It was Isaac's youngest son Charles Marshall Allcock who was to stay on in Suffolk, lodging for a time with the Whurr family in the St Mary Stoke area of Ipswich before marrying in the town and bringing up a large family.

Chapter Ten

Out to Service

The Leader's home in Gloucester Road, Horfield, Bristol where Susannah Coultas was employed. It is now a Dental Practice. (2005).

Many people in Victorian times, according to Judith Flanders, *'took having a servant as the definition for being middle class. Servants were…a symbol of status, signalling to the world the stage that the family had reached. The wife of an assistant surgeon in 1859 said: I must not do our household work, or carry my baby out: or I should lose caste. We must keep a servant.'* (1)

There was therefore a considerable market for girls to go into service, both from Ashley Down and elsewhere. Some Müller girls went into teaching or nursing, but most received training, from the age of fourteen, so that they could go out to service in due course. Through domestic science lessons they would spend some time working in the kitchens, wash houses and laundries in preparation for their future life outside. Prospective employers who wanted a servant would apply to the Müller Homes, and receive the following set of questions to be answered satisfactorily before one of the orphans could go to work for them:

Is yours a Christian family?

Are you and your husband members of an Evangelical Church?

The Directors wish the girl to attend the same place of worship which her mistress attends. Would she be allowed to do so at least once on the Lord's Day?

Is it your custom to gather your family morning and evening for reading the scriptures and prayer? And do you arrange for your servants to be present?

Of what does your family consist? How many reside at home?

Have you any besides your family residing with you?

How many rooms does your house contain?

How many servants do you keep?

What sleeping accommodation will be provided for the girl?

Is your laundry work put out or done at home? If the latter, how much do you expect the girl to do?

This degree of care and concern for the physical and spiritual welfare of those leaving Ashley Down to become servants was certainly an improvement on the notices placed by the workhouse staff on Suffolk church doors.

No child left Müller's New Orphan Houses in Bristol until employment had been found for them; the boys normally stayed at the homes until the age of fourteen and were then apprenticed, while the girls did not have to leave until they were seventeen. Most of the leavers valued the opportunities that Mr Müller had given them. In the words of one orphan, William Ready, who was at Ashley Down when the Coultas girls arrived and left in 1876:

'My belongings were my Bible, my clothes and half a crown and, best of all, was the priceless blessing of George Müller's prayers.' (2)

William Ready had been born in a London workhouse and was sleeping rough when he was 'rescued' and sent to Ashley Down aged twelve. Rebellious to start with, he settled down and went on to make good, first as an apprentice on leaving the home and later as a Free Church minister and popular preacher in New Zealand. Looking back on his years on Ashley Down, William wrote:

'I can see now that it was just the place for me and what a blessing it was that I was sent there. If my own children were left orphans I could wish for nothing better than that they should be trained and cared for at Müller's.' (3)

In 1880 Susannah Coultas reached the age of seventeen and it was therefore time for her to leave Orphan House Number Two. On September 14th, she began employment as a domestic servant with a family living close by: that of a Mr Henry Leader Junior, a clerk aged thirty-five and his wife Emma who was twenty-eight. They lived with their sons Arthur Fred and George Herbert, and their daughter Florence Maria, only a few streets away from the orphan houses, so presumably Susannah could continue to visit her younger sisters on occasion if she was allowed some time off from her work. The Leader children were still young – six, three and one year old – so maybe Susannah's duties included helping to look after them as well as domestic chores, although Mrs Leader's twenty-five year old sister Mary Coole lived with them too, so possibly she lent a hand with the children when she was not at her own work as a silk mercer's assistant.

According to the 1881 Census, Susannah's eldest sister Mary Betsy was also out to service (as presumably she had been since at least 1873), though by now some distance away in Leicester. Her employers were carpet merchant John Spurway and his wife Lucy who were both young themselves, in their mid-twenties, with a one year old son named Douglas. Mary Betsy's duties may well have included looking after him and no doubt experience of caring for her younger sisters and brothers in Suffolk while her parents were ill would have stood her in good stead for such a post.

Susannah's and Mary Betsy's employers, still relatively young, probably rented rather than owned their own homes. Judith Flanders in *The Victorian House'* says:

The Victorians as a whole found ownership of less importance than occupancy and display. Although no firm figures exist, most historians estimate that a bare ten per cent of the population owned their own homes; the rest rented: the poorest paying weekly, the prosperous middle classes taking renewable seven-year leases. This allowed families to move promptly and easily as their circumstances changed: either with the increase and decrease of the size of the family, or to larger or smaller houses in better or less good neighbourhoods as income fluctuated.' (4)

When Susannah left the orphanage the Leaders' address was Nightingale Villa, Bishopston, Bristol; by the following year they lived at 231 Gloucester Road, Horfield. It is not certain if these are one and the same or different, but if the Leaders were renting as suggested above they could well have moved a short distance to a larger property that would accommodate their growing family.

The Leader family in Bristol and the Spurways in Leicester seem to have had one servant apiece, so Susannah and Mary Betsy would have been what was known as 'maids-of-all-work' or 'general servants'. 231 Gloucester Road [still in use today but as a dental practice] appears to have had three floors, so the family would have lived on the ground and first floors, with Susannah probably living and sleeping in the basement or the scullery. At least the basement seems to have had a window mostly above ground which could let in some daylight and air. As the only servant, Susannah would have done most if not all of the manual work around the house, although her mistress may have helped with some of the tasks such as bed making or food preparation as necessary.

As Judith Flanders indicates, the turnover in servants was high, especially in households with a maid-of-all-work, with the average time in any one post being three years. For example,

Young girls from workhouses and from agricultural labourers' families often worked only for their keep in their first job, to get the training they needed in order to begin their climb up the ladder of domestic service, and also to receive the all important character reference.' (5)

Sometimes conditions were so bad they simply could not *'stay the course. One sixteen year old reported to Henry Mayhew, 'I am an orphan. When I was ten I was sent to service as a maid-of-all-work, in a small tradesman's family. It was a hard place, and my mistress used me very cruelly, beating me often. I stood my mistress's ill treatment for about six months. She beat me with sticks as well as with her hands. I was black and blue, and at last ran away.' (6)*

Fortunately not every servant fared so badly. Fifteen-year-old Hannah Winkup's experience in Suffolk in 1851 was somewhat different:

'Have been in service three quarters of a year; my mistress is very kind to me; she lived in the same village as I did; I have £2. 10s a year wages, and Missus gave me clothes worth another pound.' (7)

Nevertheless, Judith Flanders' book suggests that:

'most servants' work was backbreaking, and they were rarely healthy, suffering from long-term illnesses caused by poor nutrition, confined quarters' [often very cold and damp] 'and lack of sun and fresh air.' (8) They would be working from early morning until late in the evening when they would fall asleep from sheer exhaustion. Duties could include cleaning, sweeping and dusting, polishing, cooking and serving food, washing floors, making beds (perhaps with the mistress of the house), emptying chamber pots, washing up and scouring pans, laundry and ironing, answering the door and helping with the children. Life in Victorian households tended to be strict and ordered, with specific tasks having to be carried out on particular days of the week. For the servant, there would be little time off:

'when a half day was given, (she) was expected to get through the regular twelve hours' work by five o'clock before being allowed out. Servants rarely had Sundays off: at best, there was only a reduced workload – unless the family was one that expected an elaborate Sunday dinner.' (9)

It is not known whether Susannah and Mary Betsy were treated well or badly by their employers, although it is to be hoped that the Leaders were reasonably good to Susannah, particularly if they were the type of Christian family that Mr Müller and his co-directors sought for their orphans. What is certain is that both Mary Betsy and Susannah would have had a tough life by the standards of today. (10)

In due course Sarah Mabel was also old enough to leave the New Orphan House and go out to service. On leaving Ashley Down, like William Ready and Susannah before her, Sarah Mabel would have been provided with a set of clothes as well as a Bible and Mr Müller's blessing, and her travelling expenses would have been paid. On May 27th 1885 she travelled to the West Country to be a servant in the home of a Miss Crane who lived at La Carita, Parkstone in Dorset. This was to be Sarah's fifth place to live since her birth just seventeen years before. Her leaving record from the Müller Homes, unlike that of her two sisters, does not say that she was 'a believer'; this could have been an oversight or perhaps she was not so enthusiastic about Mr Müller's Christian message as the other girls. It is not known how long she stayed with Miss Crane, but it seems that she was one of those servants who moved on after a year or two, perhaps with a view to 'climbing the ladder of domestic service'. The 1891 Census shows her, at the age of twenty-three and still single, working as a parlour maid for John Colthurst Godwin and his wife Amelia (nee Reynolds) at The Brow, Albert Road, Clevedon in North Somerset.

John and Amelia Godwin had married at Wandsworth in 1883. John was the son of Richard Godwin of Bristol, a magistrate for the county of Somerset, and his wife Mary, and had been a lieutenant in the 2nd Somerset Militia before becoming a stockbroker. His wife Amelia was born at Simla in India, and had a son, William M Reynolds who was born in Jacobabad in India before her marriage to John Godwin. At the date of the 1891 Census, William (described as John's 'stepson') was a scholar aged twelve living with John and Amelia and their own two children, Madeline aged seven and Charles aged six, both born in London. There were two other servants in the household besides Sarah Mabel; the children's governess Amy Smith aged twenty-four and the cook Georgina Ashley, aged twenty-five. With more than one servant, class distinctions and a form of hierarchy 'below stairs' would probably have existed just as they did between employer and servants. Governesses were not much respected generally, particularly as they were not strictly speaking servants yet neither were they part of the employing family. William Makepeace Thackeray in 'Vanity Fair', published in 1848, has his character George Osborne describe Becky Sharp as '*a little nobody – a little upstart governess*' and go on to say that '*a governess is all very well but I would rather have a lady for my sister-in-law.*' The housekeeper Mrs Blenkinsop is of a similar opinion when talking to the maid: '*I don't trust them governesses, Pinner. They give themselves the hairs and hupstarts of ladies, and their wages is no better than you nor me.*' The cook was often a formidable and dominating woman, who completely ruled the roost in the kitchen, although perhaps Georgina Ashley, being only twenty-five, was not quite so set in her ways. As all three 'servants' were of a similar age, it is to be hoped that they got on reasonably well together and had at least some interests in common.

Victorian servants were usually required to wear uniform, if for no better reason than that they could be easily recognised and not mistaken for the lady of the house. Sometimes the cost of the uniform would be taken out of the girl's wages, or perhaps there would be a gift of material at Christmas, which the servant then had to make up at her own expense. In a middle-class household such as the Godwin's, parlour maid Sarah Mabel would most likely have worn a uniform of black alpaca with white lace and a neat white cap. If she went to church, as Mr Müller intended, she would have been expected to dress soberly and to sit at the back rather than with members of the family. As the '*Rules for the Manners of Servants in Good Families*' *(Ladies Sanitary Association, 1901)* showed, it was very important that all servants knew their place:

'*Always move quietly about the house, and do not let your voice be heard by the family unless necessary. Never sing or whistle at your work where the family would be likely to hear you.*

When meeting any ladies or gentlemen about the house, stand back or move aside for them to pass.

'Always speak of the children of the family as "Master" or "Miss".

'Do not smile at droll stories told in your presence, or seem in any way to notice, or enter into, the family conversation, or the talk at table, or with visitors; and do not offer any information unless asked, and then you must give it in as few words as possible. But if it is quite necessary to give some information unasked at table or before visitors, give it quietly to your master or mistress.'

Sarah Mabel must have been very familiar with rules such as these and the demanding daily routine that went with the job. Living in Clevedon not too far from Ashley Down, she may on her 'day off' have been able to meet up with old friends from the Müller Homes. It was also a pleasant place to live, being a Victorian seaside resort on the Bristol Channel; time off might have included a walk to the Victorian pier or listening to music by the bandstand, both of which were not far from Albert Road and are still standing today. It is not known what became of Sarah Mabel after working for the Godwins, as there is no record of her after 1891. She may have climbed the ladder of service, married and had children of her own or, of course, like so many other members of her family, she might have died young.

Servants taking a break from hard work for a photograph. Their dress is typical of the late Victorian period when Mary Betsy, Susannah and Sarah Mabel Coultas were in service.

Chapter Eleven

Marriages and Beyond

Susannah Gill (nee Coultas) at her daughter's christening. The baby is thought to be Gertrude Daisy, born in 1891.

1882 was a year when the Coultas family had, at last, some cause for celebration. Mary Betsy was to leave service with Mr and Mrs Spurway in Leicester to marry Samuel Austin, an ostler from Bulwell in Nottinghamshire. Their marriage took place on April 17th that year at the parish church in Bulwell. It would have been held in the morning [hence a 'wedding breakfast']; it was not until 1886 that weddings could by law take place after 12 noon. Perhaps Mary Betsy's surviving sisters Susannah, Sarah Mabel and Louisa Charlotte travelled from Bristol to be there, possibly as bridesmaids, at least for that special day. (1) Bulwell was presumably chosen as it was not only the bridegroom's village but also the former home of Mary Betsy's maternal grandparents, Thomas Austin and his wife Mary (*nee* Hallam). Thomas was working as a gamekeeper at Bulwell Hall in 1873, although by 1881 he and Mary appear to have moved to Woolaton in another part of Nottingham. One of Mary Betsy's uncles, Philip Austin, was a witness to the marriage; the other witness was Annie Maria Shipp, who was the cook in a small boarding school in Nottingham but had been born at Occold in Suffolk. She could have been one of Mary Betsy's friends when she lived in the county [Annie Shipp was about three years older] or maybe they had been in service together at some stage. Samuel Austin is thought to have been Mary Betsy's cousin, the illegitimate son of her aunt, Elizabeth Brown (*nee* Austin). This sounds rather complicated, with the bride's grandparents, uncle and aunt all sharing the same surname as her bridegroom.

Mary Betsy and Samuel settled in Bulwell where they brought up six children of their own: Herbert (born 1883), Eliza, presumably named after Mary Betsy's mother (born 1886), Arthur (born 1888), Florence (born 1891), Nellie (born 1898) and Annie (born 1901). Samuel continued to work with horses, being described on the 1901 Census as a coal horse keeper, underground worker, no doubt in the Nottinghamshire coal mines. It seems appropriate that he had married a 'keeper of colts'!

The family's delight on the occasion of Mary Betsy's wedding was once again to be short lived. In the summer of 1883, youngest sister Louisa Charlotte died of consumption while she was still at the Müller Orphan Houses, aged just thirteen. What sadness there must have been amongst her family and friends and the staff at Ashley Down. Of the seven Coultas children who had begun life so happily in Suffolk, only three were still alive. Within a few more years, news would also reach them of the death of another Benhall cousin, Isaac Allcock, in 1886, and of his father Isaac on November 27th 1887, aged 61.

My grandmother Susannah waited until she was twenty-seven – relatively late in those days –before deciding to marry. Her husband, William Goodall Gill, had been born in Bagthorpe, a small hamlet close to Selston in Nottinghamshire where their wedding took place on October 8th 1890. The rector who would have taken the service was a Rev Charles Harrison. I had often wondered about the significance of William's middle name, but it appears that he was named after an uncle called William Goodall. It is interesting that both Mary Betsy Coultas and Susannah Coultas found husbands in Nottinghamshire although they lived and worked elsewhere. This suggests that they – and their parents when they were alive – continued to maintain strong links with their relatives in the

Nottingham area all the time they were in Suffolk or out to service in other parts of the country.

Susannah Gill (nee Coultas) with her husband William and their five daughters: Daisy, Lily, Mabel (MEG), Winnie and Annie. Probably taken at Annie's christening 1904.

Throughout their married life, Susannah and William lived at The White House, Bagthorpe, where they brought up their young family of five girls:

Gertrude Daisy Gill known as Daisy (1891–1959). She married Samuel Redgate and had seven children.
Lillian Ada Gill known as Lily (1893–1963). She married Willis Sowter Todd but had no children.
My mother, Mabel Ethel Gill known by her initials as Meg (1894–1972), married Arthur George Tunnell. Presumably she was named in honour of her aunt, Sarah Mabel Coultas.
Winifred May Gill known as Winnie (1897–1982). She married Robert Bond. Their son Frederic Coultas Bond was brought up by his Aunt Lily and Uncle Willis at Bleak Hall Farm, Kirkby in Ashfield.
Annie Elizabeth Gill (1904–1967). Annie was my godmother, after whom I was christened Anne. She never married.

Mary Betsy and Susannah both named their youngest daughters 'Annie'. It would seem likely that this was in recognition of the care their aunt Ann, or

Annie Allcock, had shown to her brother's family in Suffolk while she was alive. Three of the Gill sisters married farmers and Winnie's son Fred also farmed, carrying on the family tradition of husbandry begun by Robert Coultas in Yorkshire as far back as 1811 and continued by his son George in Lincolnshire for many years. (2) It became another Gill family tradition that the eldest child in each branch of the family would bear the Coultas name in honour of Susannah, so 'Coultas' lives on in my own name and that of some of my Nottinghamshire cousins.

William Gill was a builder who, according to these cousins, built (or at least helped to build) Underwood Church, near to Selston and Bagthorpe, in the 1890s. Nearby was Newstead Abbey, the home of the poet Lord Byron (1788-1824), who, in my mother's eyes, was definitely a local hero. I doubt though if she had any idea of his scandalous reputation, and she certainly knew nothing about his daughter Ada being credited with being the first computer programmer! After William's death, Susannah moved to Kirkby in Ashfield – about five miles from Bagthorpe – where she died in 1944. I remember as a small child being at the back of her red-brick Victorian house when a charming man came to talk to me over the garden fence. The 'charming man' turned out to be Max Wall, the actor and comedian renowned for his funny walk, who regularly stayed for the summer theatre season in the house next door.

Susannah's daughter Meg nursed at hospitals in Nottingham, Derby and Guildford, making a name for herself as a theatre sister before marrying my father, Arthur Tunnell, at Selston Church (like her mother before her) in 1933. Arthur's first wife, Agnes, had become ill with tuberculosis – it evidently ran on both sides of my family – and my mother nursed her until her death. Meg was skilled at cooking and needlework and a regular church-goer all her life. Perhaps these were legacies that Susannah passed on as a result of her years in the New Orphan House at Ashley Down. Meg hated housework however, and always had a 'daily' to tackle the domestic chores; another legacy of Susannah's long hours in service maybe! Arthur was well respected in the community, and my mother and I were very proud when, in recognition of his many years in insurance and voluntary work including the British Red Cross Society, he was appointed MBE in 1955.

Charles Marshall Allcock, the youngest of Ann and Isaac's children, continued to live in Suffolk and went to work in Ipswich. He married Alice Gertrude Kemp and they had ten children, most or all of whom were born in Ipswich. These were Blanche Eleanor (date of birth unknown but said to have died very young in a fire) Mabel (date of birth unknown, died Ipswich 1891), Florence (born about 1887), Rosa Marion (born about 1889), Alice (born about 1890), Robert Isaac (born about 1893), Charles Marshall junior (born 1896), Arthur Edward (born 1898), George Alfred (born 1899) and Eleanor Louise (born June 10th 1903 at 105 Harland Street, Ipswich, died 1988). In 2004 I was delighted to make contact with one of the descendants of Charles Marshall Allcock senior and his daughter Eleanor Louise (and therefore one of my distant cousins) through the internet. From him I learned that Charles worked at the Ransomes & Rapier Foundry, formed as a separate company from Ransomes, Sims and Jefferies in 1868 to handle the production of railway equipment, where he was injured and lost an eye. For some unknown reason Charles had the nickname of 'Day Day'. He later moved to Richmond in Surrey where he worked at the lock and died there on November 5th 1945.

Charles Marshall Allcock, son of Ann and Isaac Allcock of Benhall, nicknamed 'Day Day'. He and his cousin Susannah Coultas were born within a few months of each other in 1863.

Passenger trains continued to run on the Great Eastern Railway branch line into Framlingham until November 3rd 1952, while freight trains used the line until 1963. This was the year of the Beeching Report into British Railways which was to change the face of the rail network throughout the country. Wickham Market still has no station of its own except in name; trains running daily between Ipswich and Lowestoft continue to stop at Campsea Ashe, though the station house is now privately owned. Wickham Market workhouse closed in 1936 but had a variety of uses after that. Today it is in residential use and known as 'Deben Court'. Parham School celebrated its centenary in 1973 but was closed on July 18th 1986.

In Bristol Mr Müller's son-in-law, James Wright, looked after things at Ashley Down very capably while George was abroad, though they were both greatly saddened by the death of James's wife Lydia in 1890 and by the passing of Susannah Müller in 1894. George Müller himself died in March 1898 at the ripe old age of ninety-two and his funeral procession brought much of Bristol to a standstill (3), with thousands lining the route. The New Orphan Houses closed as such in 1958 and became the property of the Local Education Authority; more than 18,000 children had been cared for since Müller opened his first home in 1835. Today the houses are part of the City of Bristol College (and sometimes used as a film set for BBC1's *Casualty* and *Holby City Hospital*) but Mr Müller's Christian work of supporting children in need goes on within the community. Muller Road and Muller Avenue, in the Ashley Down area of the city, and The George Müller Foundation with its museum, are tributes to his memory and to the vision of a remarkable man.

By 1876 the Rev Edwin Watkins had left Benhall but remained in Suffolk to become the vicar of St Peter's Church at Ubbeston, six miles from Halesworth. He succeeded to the living on the death of the Rev Robert James, the first resident vicar of Ubbeston and, like Edwin Watkins, a former CMS missionary in the diocese of Rupert's Land in Canada. The living was in the gift of the Rev Edmund Holland MA of Benhall Lodge, as was that of Benhall, so Mr Holland must have been instrumental in procuring this position for Edwin Watkins. His vicarage was originally a small house that dated from 1776 and had been purchased originally from Gerard Vanneck, Lord Huntingfield, who within a couple of years was to start rebuilding the nearby mansion of Heveningham Hall. Extensions to the parsonage over the years made it more substantial and elegant and it became a rectory in 1847. (4) Described by White as a *'commodious vicarage house'* in 1885, it had seven acres of glebe land to go with it. (5)

Edwin Watkins seems to have been a man who liked to get things done, so it is not surprising that throughout his time in Ubbeston, alterations and repairs to the Church, which could seat 150 people, were being carried out. The interior was restored and reseated in 1865, with further restorations of the exterior and the windows being made in 1878 at a cost of £253 and again in 1892 at a cost of £100. (6)

He was also, it appears, a generous man. From 1876, for the next thirty years, the Church accounts show a succession of gifts from the Rev Watkins and his family to the church and the parish, including a pipe organ to replace Robert James' harmonium, and a beef and plum pudding dinner for every family to celebrate Queen Victoria's Golden Jubilee in 1887. (7) Edwin's wife Ann predeceased him in 1888 aged sixty-five but he continued to live at Ubbeston with his two unmarried daughters. His son Arthur, born at Fort George, had by then qualified as a civil engineer and on the 1901 Census was to be found, aged forty-three, living at Greenwich in London.

Like the Coultas and Allcock families before him, the Rev Watkins was to experience the death of a child during his lifetime, when his daughter Ellen Georgina died at the age of 37 in 1899. Then in 1907, at the age of 78, Edwin set off one day on his bicycle to visit parishioners and was found dead at the top of Clay Hill, within sight of the church which he had served for thirty-one years. (8) It was an abrupt end to what had been a long and dedicated career, in Canada and Suffolk, as a Christian clergyman. (9) His successor as vicar, the Rev Alfred Jugge Bedell, was to reside outside the village at Cratfield, but Edwin's elder daughter Alice continued to live in Ubbeston until her death in 1935. Four years later the Rectory was sold and in 1974 the church itself was converted into a private house. Interior furnishings and at least one bell were moved to other churches in Suffolk, including Heveningham and Henley near Ipswich, but the fine late medieval red brick tower remains.

A little of the Suffolk dialect, which intrigued Agnes Strickland around 150 years ago, must have passed by word of mouth from Susannah to me, as I recognise and even use some of the unique words and phrases that are seldom heard today. *'Airy-wiggle'*, for example, meaning an ear-wig; *'cuckoo spit'* for the white froth seen on hedgerows and leaves in spring; a *'deal'* – a large amount; *'Fair to middlin'* – a state of reasonable health; *'gos-gogs'* for gooseberries and *'lords and ladies'* for wild arum; *'fusty'* meaning musty, mildew, smelly; *'nous/nows'* for clever, able, understanding; *'proper poorly'* meaning extremely unwell and *'worry guts'* for someone who is very anxious. (10) I thought nothing of these phrases as a child; I now realise they may well have originated in Suffolk.

The story of Susannah Coultas in Suffolk is one of 'a life unnoticed'. Like so many people in rural areas over the generations, she and her family were neither famous nor outstanding, but their pathway through life and death deserves to be recorded; without them my cousins and I would not be here. James and Eliza, Ann and Isaac and their families lived in Suffolk for a relatively short period, through good times and bad. Yet Susannah, having overcome great adversity in her young life, took great pride in her Suffolk roots and passed this on to my mother Meg and in turn to me. I love to explore Snape and Framlingham, with the villages in between, and try to visualise what life was like for my relatives living there in Victorian times.

I have been privileged to have many opportunities in my own life, yet it is unlikely that they would have been possible had not the Rev Edwin Watkins of Benhall and Mr George Müller of Bristol – both pioneering and inspirational men in their different ways – made such a significant difference to the life of Susannah Coultas. I owe them a debt of gratitude. Having now lived in the county for more than forty years, I am proud to say 'My grandmother was born in Suffolk'.

Five Generations of the Coultas Family

1. Robert Coultas

Born 1786, Wykeham,
Yorkshire;
died 1854

married **Ann Marshall** in 1811 at North Grimston, Yorkshire.

Children of Robert and Ann Coultas (*nee* Marshall):

John Coultas	born 1812 North Grimston Yorkshire; died 1871 Nottinghamshire, married Louisa Ellis
Robert Coultas	born 1815 North Grimston, died Eastwood, Nottinghamshire, 1836
George Coultas	born 1817 North Grimston, lived Lincolnshire; died 1898
Susannah Coultas	born 1818 North Grimston; died 1818
Thomas Coultas	born 1819 North Grimston; died before 1873?
William Coultas	born 1821 North Grimston
Susannah Coultas	born 1823 North Grimston; died 1885, married Thomas Clifford
Mary Ann Coultas	born 1825 Greasley Nottinghamshire, married William Ellis
Charles Coultas	born 1827 Greasley; died 1832

2. Ann Coultas

born 1829 Greasley;
died 1880 Suffolk,
married <u>Isaac Allcock,</u> lived Benhall Suffolk

Henry Coultas	born 1831 Greasley; died 1836

2. James Coultas born 1833, Greasley;
died Suffolk 1873;
married <u>Eliza Hallam</u>, lived Framlingham,
Parham, Farnham, Suffolk

Marshall Coultas	born 1835 Greasley; died 1836

Eliza Coultas born 1837 Arnold Nottinghamshire,
married John Salmon

Children of James and Eliza Coultas (*nee* Hallam):

Mary Betsy Coultas born 1859 Framlingham Suffolk
married Samuel Austin, lived Bulwell
Nottinghamshire

Eliza Ann Coultas born 1861 Parham Suffolk,
died 1876 Benhall, Suffolk

3. Susannah Coultas

born 1863 Farnham Suffolk;
died 1944;
married <u>William Goodall</u> <u>Gill</u>; lived
Bagthorpe Nottinghamshire

Robert Haythorne Coultas born 1865 Farnham Suffolk;
died 1878 Langton, Lincolnshire

Sarah Mabel Coultas born 1868 Farnham Suffolk

Louisa Charlotte Coultas born 1869 Farnham Suffolk;
died 1883 Gloucestershire

John Henry Coultas born 1871 Farnham Suffolk;
died 1873 Framlingham Suffolk

Children of Ann (*nee* Coultas) and Isaac Allcock:

Robert Allcock   born 1849 Nottinghamshire

Isaac Allcock   born 1851 Derbyshire;
                           died 1886

George Allcock   born 1852;
                           died Benhall, Suffolk, 1859

Ann/e Allcock   born 1854 Hereford

Alice Allcock   born 1858 Benhall Suffolk

John George Allcock   born 1861;
                           died Benhall, 1862

3. Charles Marshall Allcock
                           born 1863 Benhall Suffolk;
                           married <u>Alice Gertrude Kemp</u>,
                           died Richmond Surrey, 1945

Children of Susannah (*nee* Coultas) and William Goodall Gill:

Gertrude Daisy Gill   born 1891 Bagthorpe Nottinghamshire;
                           died 1959

Lillian Ada Gill   born 1893 Bagthorpe;
                           died 1963

4. Mabel Ethel Gill   born 1894 Bagthorpe;
                           died 1972;
                           married **Arthur George Tunnell**

Winifred May Gill   born 1897 Bagthorpe; died 1982

Annie Elizabeth Gill   born 1904 Bagthorpe; died 1967

Only child of Mabel Ethel (*nee* Gill) and Arthur George Tunnell:

5. Anne Coultas Tunnell
                           born 1935 Merrow, Guildford Surrey
                           (the author)

Appendix Two

Relatives of the orphaned children of James and Eliza Coultas. List made prior to admission of the children to The New Orphan Houses, Bristol (1873–1874)

Maternal **Grandfather** Thomas Austin +   Game Keeper
Maternal **Grandmother** Mrs (Mary) Austin   Bulwell Hall,
                                               Nottinghamshire

Paternal Grandfather & Grandmother deceased

Uncles and Aunts:

Ann Allcock (nee Coultas)   Benhall Saxmundham,
                                   Suffolk
Isaac Allcock +   Great Eastern Railway
                                   Servant, Benhall,
                                   Saxmundham Suffolk

Thomas Austin +   Hebburn Colliery, Durham

Henry Austin +   23 Danville Street Sheffield

John Austin +   23 Danville Street Sheffield

(John) Brown   Walk Mill, Papplewick,
                                   Nottinghamshire
Elizabeth Brown + (*nee* Austin)   Walk Mill, Papplewick,
                                   Nottinghamshire

George Coultas +   Farmer, Langton near
                                   Wragby, Lincolnshire

John Salmon +   Collier

Eliza Salmon (*nee* Coultas)   Newthorpe, Nottingham

William Ellis
Mary Ellis (*nee* Coultas)   Labourers, Trent Bridge,
                                   Gatehouse, Nottingham

Stephen Austin   Pilsley, Derbyshire

Philip Austin   'At home with his parents'

Thomas Clifford   Farm Labourer
Susannah Clifford (*nee* Coultas)   Hermitage Farm, Green Hill
                                      Lane, Derbyshire

+ = Those relatives who agreed in December 1873 *'that in case of any unforeseen circumstance whatsoever, the orphans Susannah Coultas, Sarah Mabel Coultas and Louisa Charlotte Coultas should need to be dismissed from the New Orphan Houses on Ashley Down, Bristol, we will receive them till they can be admitted into the Wickham Work House.'* (*Coultas Admission and Dismissal Records and Family File,* The George Müller Foundation*)*

References

A Dictionary of British Surnames. P H Reaney, Routledge & Kegan Paul, 1958.

History, Gazetteer, and Directory of Suffolk. William White, 1844.

Suffolk in the Nineteenth Century. The Actual Condition of Suffolk in 1851, John Glyde Junior.

Post Office Directory of Suffolk. 1858. Suffolk Record Office.

Morris's Directory of Suffolk with Great Yarmouth and Newmarket. 1868. Suffolk Record Office, ref. S058.

A History, Gazetteer & Directory of Suffolk. William White, 1874.

A History of Suffolk, by David Dymond & Peter Northeast, published in 1985 by Phillimore & Co. Ltd, Shopwyke Manor Barn, Chichester, West Sussex, PO20 2BG. Reproduced by kind permission.

The Workhouse: Wickham Market, Suffolk. E P Cockburn, 1991.

Minutes of the Wickham Market Work House, Plomesgate Union Suffolk: December 1873 to March 13th 1876. Suffolk Record Office, ref. ADA6/AB1/10.

Rev Edwin Watkins: Missionary to the Cree: 1852–1857. John S Long. (www.nipissingu.ca/ faculty/johnlo/ john_long)

The Bristol Miracle. The George Müller Foundation. (www.mullers.org)

Rural Robustness – health and medicine in the nineteenth century countryside. Lori Williamson Ph. D., Sep 2001. (www.berksfhs.org.uk)

Extracts from *Of Human Bondage.* W Somerset Maugham published by Heinemann, 1915. Used by permission of The Random House Group Limited.

Sir Robert Hitcham's Primary School's website, (www.hitchams.suffolk.sch.uk). College Road, Framlingham.

Larn yarself Silly Suffolk. David Woodward, Nostalgia Publications, 1997.

The Victorian Railway Worker. Trevor May, Shire Publications Ltd. Cromwell House, Church Street, Princes Risborough HP27 9AA, 2003.

The Victorian House. Judith Flanders, Harper Perennial, an imprint of HarperCollins Publishers, 77-85 Fulham Palace Road, Hammersmith London, 2003.

Coultas Admission and Dismissal Records and Family File. The George Müller Foundation, Müller House, 7 Cotham Park, Bristol.

Lost Railways of East Anglia. Leslie Oppitz, Countryside Books, 2003. (www.countrysidebooks.co.uk)

Suffolk Bedside Book: A collection of Prose and Poetry. Selected and Introduced by Clive Paine, The Dovecote Press, (dovecotepress@btinternet.com), 2002.

Hodskinson's Map of Suffolk in 1783. Larks Press, Ordnance Farmhouse, Guist Bottom, Dereham Norfolk NR20 5PF, January 2003.

English Villagers: Life in the Countryside. Valerie Porter, Bounty Books, a division of Octopus Publishing Group Limited, 2004. First published in 1992 by George Philip Limited.

Eating with the Victorians. Edited by C. Anne Wilson, paperback edition, 2004. Chapter 7 – *Supper: The Ultimate Meal* by C. Anne Wilson, Sutton Publishing Ltd., Phoenix Mill, Thrupp, Stroud, Gloucestershire GL5 2BU.

The Biography of a Victorian Village. Richard Cobbold's account of Wortham, Suffolk 1860. Edited and Introduced by Ronald Fletcher, B T Batsford Ltd. London, 1977.

Kelly's Directory of Suffolk. 1908.

Parham School Committee Minute Book 1872-1903. Suffolk Record Office. Ref. FC110/M1/1.

The Old Rectory, Ubbeston in *The Poaching Priors of Blythburgh.* Veronica Baker-Smith, Blythburgh, 2002.

Delighted in God, A Biography of George Müller. Roger Steer, Christian Focus Publications Ltd, Geanies House, Fearn, Tain, Ross-shire IV20 1TW, 1997.

List of Photographs and Illustrations

- Front Cover: Houses in the Street, Parham; Farnham Church; Snape Bridge; Framlingham Castle. (Photos: the author).
- Back Cover: Susannah Coultas and daughter. (Photo in the author's possession).
- St Nicholas Church, North Grimston, Yorkshire. (Photo: Jeff and Dorothy Bradbury).
- North Grimston Church, Chancel Arch and Font. (Photos: John Salmon).
- Framlingham Castle 1904. (Photo: Suffolk Record Office, ref. K681/1/170/7).
- Interior of Parham Church. (Photo: the author).
- Map of Suffolk Towns and Railways. (Reproduced with permission of Phillimore & Co. Ltd.).
- Map of Parham village showing the railway, 1883. (Reproduced from 1883 Ordnance Survey map, with permission. Suffolk Record Office, ref. 59/1 and 59/2).
- Parham Station. Circa 1900. (Photo: Suffolk Record Office, ref. K681/1/355/23).
- Steam train at the station. (Photo: Reproduced with permission of Sir Robert Hitcham's Primary School, Framlingham).
- Hodskinson's Map of Suffolk in 1783, showing the villages where the Coultas and Allcock families lived. (Reproduced with permission of Larks Press).
- Cree Communities of Quebec: Map showing James' Bay with Fort George and Chisasibi. (Reproduced with permission of Brian Back/Ottertooth.com)
- Cree Syllabics, Canada. (Reproduced with permission of Simon Ager).
- Scenes at Chisasibi, (formerly Fort George), Quebec. (Photos: L&G Development Corporation, Brockville, Ontario, Canada).
- George Müller, founder of the New Orphan Homes, Ashley Down, Bristol. (Photo: reproduced with permission of the George Müller Foundation).
- Deben Court, formerly Wickham Market Workhouse. (Photo: Peter Higginbotham/ www.workhouses.org.uk).
- Letter from the Rev E A Watkins to the New Orphan Homes, 1874. (Coultas Family File).
- Müller's five Orphan Houses, Ashley Down, Bristol. (Photo: The George Müller Foundation; reproduced with permission).

- Müller's New Orphan House Number One, Ashley Down, 2004. (Photo: the author)
- Müller girls on their annual outing to Purdown (Photo: The George Müller Foundation; reproduced with permission).
- Illustrations from 'Marion and her Cousins' by F Scarlett Potter, SPCK. (Book in the author's possession).
- The Leaders' house in Gloucester Road, Horfield, Bristol, 2004, now a Dental Practice. (Photo: Chris Dunford, with permission of Oasis Dental Care, Bishopston).
- Servants taking a break for a photograph. (Photo in the author's possession).
- Susannah Coultas with daughter, probably 1891. (Photo in the author's possession).
- Susannah (*nee* Coultas) and William Gill at Bagthorpe with their five daughters, probably 1904. (Photo in the author's possession).
- Charles Marshall Allcock. (Photo: reproduced with permission of Lois Samuels and Jeff Taylor-Jackson).

Notes

Chapter One: Introduction – Journey to Suffolk

Chapter Two: Family Origins

1.   See <u>Appendix One</u>: Five Generations of the Coultas Family. There were many Coultas and Marshall families in Yorkshire at the time, so it has been difficult to identify the parents of Robert Coultas and Ann Marshall. It is, however, very probable that Robert was the son of George Coultas (born 1757) and Mary (*nee* Simpkin) (born 1756), who married at Ganton parish church on December 16th 1779, and that Ann was the daughter of John Marshall and Susannah (*nee* Etty), baptised on April 11th 1796 at North Grimston. Robert and his four brothers and four sisters were all baptised at Wykeham. Generations of the Coultas family in this part of Yorkshire have been traced back, with reasonable certainty, to 1707

2.   Reaney P H. *A Dictionary of British Surnames*. 1958.

3.   See <u>Appendix One</u>: Five Generations of the Coultas Family.

4.   Woodward, David. *Larn yarself Silly Suffolk*. 1997. Page 37.

5.   Payne, Clive. *Suffolk Bedside Book*. 2002. Pages 89–90.

6.   Dymond, David and Northeast, Peter. *A History of Suffolk*. 1985. Page 90.

7.   *Ibid.* Page 93.

8.   Payne, Clive. *Suffolk Bedside Book*. 2002. Page 29.

9.   *Ibid.*

Chapter Three: Work on the Railways

1.   May, Trevor. *The Victorian Railway Worker*. 2003. Page 10.

2.   Payne, Clive. *Suffolk Bedside Book, 2002*. Page 76.

3.   *Ibid*, page 77.

4.   White, William. *History, Gazeteer, and Directory of Suffolk*. 1844.

5.   *Ibid.*

6.   Glyde Junior, John. *Suffolk in the Nineteenth Century*. 1851.

7.   White, William. *A History, Gazetteer & Directory of Suffolk*. 1874.

8.   *Ibid.*

9.   Oppitz, Leslie. *Lost Railways of East Anglia*. 2003. Pages 10–11.

10.   May, Trevor. *The Victorian Railway Worker*. Page 6.

11.   Glyde Junior, John. *Suffolk in the Nineteenth Century*. 1851

12.   May, Trevor. *The Victorian Railway Worker*. Page 25.

13.   Dymond, David and Northeast, Peter. *A History of Suffolk*. 1985. Page 101 and See <u>Map of Suffolk Towns and Railways</u>, reproduced from page 102.

14.   Payne, Clive. *Suffolk Bedside Book, 2002*. Page 151.

15.   Dymond, David and Northeast, Peter. *A History of Suffolk*. 1985. Pages 101–102.

16.   Oppitz, Leslie. *Lost Railways of East Anglia*. 2003. Page 108.

17.   *Post Office Directory of Suffolk*. 1858.

18.   Sir Robert Hitcham's Primary School, Framlingham website: (<u>www.hitchams.suffolk.sch.uk</u>)

19.   May, Trevor. *The Victorian Railway Worker*. Page 17.

20.   *Ibid.*

21.   *Ibid.* Pages 17–18

22.   Oppitz, Leslie. *Lost Railways of East Anglia*. 2003. Page 109.

23.   *Ibid.* Page 110.

24.   Porter, Valerie. *English Villagers: Life in the Countryside.* 1992, republished in 2004. Page 42.

25.   May, Trevor. *The Victorian Railway Worker.* Page 10.

26.   *Ibid.*

27.   *Ibid.*

28.   *Ibid.* Page 29.

29.   *Ibid.*

Chapter Four: Family Life

1.   Flanders, Judith. *The Victorian House.* 2003. Page 14.

2.   *Ibid.* Page 16.

3.   Williamson, Lori. *Rural Robustness – health and medicine in the nineteenth century countryside.* September 2001.

4.   *Ibid.*

5.   *Hodskinson's Map of Suffolk in 1783.* 2003.

6.   *Morris's Directory of Suffolk with Great Yarmouth.* 1868.

7.   *Ibid.* and White, William. *A History, Gazetteer & Directory of Suffolk.* 1874.

8.   Cobbold, Richard. *The Biography of a Victorian Village.* 1860. Ed. 1977.

9.   Porter, Valerie. *English Villagers: Life in the Countryside.* 1992, republished in 2004. Page 23.

10.   Cobbold, Richard. *The Biography of a Victorian Village.* 1860. Ed. 1977.

11.   Payne, Clive. *Suffolk Bedside Book.* 2002. Pages 111–112.

12.   Dymond, David and Northeast, Peter. *A History of Suffolk.* 1985. Page 104.

13. *Morris's Directory of Suffolk with Great Yarmouth.* 1868. and White, William. *A History, Gazetteer & Directory of Suffolk.* 1874.

14. White, William. *A History, Gazetteer & Directory of Suffolk.* 1874.

15. *Parham School Committee Minute Book,* 1872–1903.

16. Plomesgate Hundred and Union comprised 41 Suffolk parishes including Benhall, Farnham, Parham and Wickham Market.

17. Payne, Clive. *Suffolk Bedside Book, 2002.* Pages 72-75.

18. *Ibid.* Page 74.

19. Woodward, David. *Larn yarself Silly Suffolk.* 1997. Page 50.

20. Wilson, C. Anne (Ed.) *Eating with the Victorians.* 2004. Pages 147–148.

21. Porter, Valerie. *English Villagers: Life in the Countryside.* 1992, republished in 2004. Page 115.

22. *Morris's Directory of Suffolk with Great Yarmouth.* 1868.

23. White, William. *A History, Gazetteer & Directory of Suffolk.* 1874.

24. Porter, Valerie. *English Villagers: Life in the Countryside.* 1992, republished in 2004. Page 115.

25. White, William. *A History, Gazetteer & Directory of Suffolk.* 1874.

Chapter Five: Change of Fortune

1. Williamson, Lori. *Rural Robustness – health and medicine in the nineteenth century countryside.* September 2001.

2. *Ibid.*

3. Glyde Junior, John. *Suffolk in the Nineteenth Century.* 1851.

4. Maugham, W Somerset. *Of Human Bondage.* 1915. Pages 459–460.

5. Williamson, Lori. *Rural Robustness – health and medicine in the nineteenth century countryside.* September 2001.

6.   Flanders, Judith. *The Victorian House*. 2003. Pages 40–41.

Chapter Six.   Curate to the Rescue

1.   George Müller Foundation. *Coultas Admission and Dismissal Records and Family File.*

2.   Rev Edwin Arthur Watkins was born on March 17th 1827, the youngest child of John Watkins, yeoman. Educated at Walsall Grammar School in Staffordshire, he was apprenticed for six years as a druggist and chemist with C Watkins, Chemist, High Street, Walsall before applying on February 24th 1848 to enter the missionary service. He had some Greek and Latin, although his attainments were not extensive, as well as slight Hebrew and some French. He was recommended to the Islington Institute (CMS Training College) by the Rev J H Harwoods, vicar of Walsall, who had known him for three years. He married Ann Cowley (daughter of Thomas Cowley, coach harness manufacturer) on April 14th 1852 at the parish church of Rushall, Staffordshire; they were both then residing at Rushall Hall. Within a couple of months the newly weds had set off for their voyage to Canada, arriving at Moose Factory on August 15th. At one time Ann Cowley was thought to be related to one of the archdeacons in the diocese of Rupert's Land (either archdeacon Cockran or archdeacon Abraham Cowley) but this was incorrect and due to the confusion between the Cowley names.

3.   Long, John S. *Rev Edwin Watkins: Missionary to the Cree: 1852–1857*. For a detailed account of Rev Watkins' missionary work with the Cree in Canada, see John Long's excellent paper, available on his website. (www.nipissingu.ca/faculty/johnlo/john_long)

4.   *Ibid.*

5.   *Ibid.*

6.   *Ibid.*

7.   *Ibid.*

8.   Mapleton was north east of Winnipeg and just south of modern-day Selkirk. The area, on Red River, was also known as Sugar Point because of the maple trees that grew there. Cumberland House, on an island in the Saskatchewan River delta, was the oldest permanent settlement in

Saskatchewan, established as an inland post of the HBC in 1774. Known in the Cree dialect as *'Waskahikanihk'*, it lies eighty-five miles north east of Nipawin. 'Nipowewin' meant 'standing place' or 'waiting place' – the place where Indian women and children stood, watched and waited as their husbands and sons paddled away by canoe, travelling hundreds of miles in terrifying waters. The Devon mission was founded in 1840 by catechist Henry Budd, the first native Indian to be ordained. Edwin Watkins ordered supplies for Mr Budd and presumably worked with him. Originally the Devon mission was called Cumberland Station, near the mouth of the Pasquia River and some fifty miles from Cumberland House. Rev Watkins, in a letter to the CMS in 1861, referred to the confusion between the two Cumberlands and to solve the problem Bishop Anderson renamed it Devon. Later it became known as The Pas which is across the border from Cumberland House in present-day Manitoba.

Further papers on the history of the Anglican Church in Canada are available on the Manitoba Historical Society's website www.mhs.mb.ca/docs and from the Church Missionary Society archives in Birmingham, England. (P.Bassett@bham.ac.uk)

9. Long, John S. *Rev Edwin Watkins: Missionary to the Cree: 1852–1857.*

10. In his haste to take action on the children's behalf, Rev Watkins initially misunderstood the number who needed to be found a new home. John Henry Coultas, the youngest of James' and Eliza's seven children, was dead by this time, and Mary Betsy and Eliza Ann (the two older girls) were 'out at service', so there were in fact four orphans, not five, in need of somewhere to live.

11. The George Müller Foundation. *Coultas Admission and Dismissal Records and Family File.*

Chapter Seven. The Müller Homes

1. Steer, Roger. *Delighted in God, A Biography of George Müller.* 1997. Pages 91–92.

2. *Ibid.* Page 97.

3. *Ibid.* Page 113.

4.   The George Müller Foundation. *The Bristol Miracle.*

5.   The George Müller Foundation. *Coultas Admission and Dismissal Records and Family File.*

6.   Steer, Roger. *Delighted in God, A Biography of George Müller.* 1997. Pages 154–155.

7.   The George Müller Foundation. *Coultas Admission and Dismissal Records and Family File.*

8.   The George Müller Foundation. *The Bristol Miracle.*

9.   The certificates included relevant birth, marriage and death certificates, and also smallpox vaccination certificates for the three Coultas girls. Although Susannah and Louisa Charlotte had been vaccinated as infants, it appears that this had been overlooked for Sarah Mabel. She had therefore to be vaccinated in December 1873 at the age of six, presumably as a pre-requisite for admission to the Müller Homes.

10.   The George Müller Foundation. *Coultas Admission and Dismissal Records and Family File.*

11.   *Ibid.*

12.   Steer, Roger. *Delighted in God, A Biography of George Müller.* 1997. Page 57.

13.   Langton by Wragby was roughly equidistant from Lincoln and Horncastle, a small rural village noted for being the birthplace of Archbishop of Canterbury Stephen Langton (1156-1228). Stephen, the son of Henry Langton Lord of the Manor of Langton by Wragby, was responsible for mediating between King John and his barons to achieve the signing of the Magna Carta in 1215, and was also the person who first divided the Bible into chapters in 1228.

14.   See Appendix One.

15.   Maugham, W Somerset. *Of Human Bondage.* 1915. Extracts from pages 5–14.

16.   See Appendix Two: List of Coultas Relatives sent to George Müller. Other Coultas uncles [see Appendix One] were dead by this time, except

perhaps for William Coultas (born in 1821). He was apparently alive, with a wife and at least one daughter, and living in Lancashire. Perhaps the family had lost touch or could not get hold of him quickly enough to sign the form. Whatever the reason, he is not mentioned as a relative in the Müller Homes family file. There may also have been another uncle on the Austin side of the family – Samuel Austin born about 1850 – but again he is not referred to in the List.

17.   The George Müller Foundation. *Coultas Admission and Dismissal Records and Family File.*

18.   *Ibid.*

19.   Steer, Roger. *Delighted in God, A Biography of George Müller.* 1997. Page 153.

Chapter Eight: A Setback

1.   White, William. *History, Gazeteer, and Directory of Suffolk.* 1844.

2.   Cockburn, E P. *The Workhouse: Wickham Market, Suffolk.* 1991.

3.   *Ibid.* Page 4.

4.   *Ibid.* Page 6.

5.   The George Müller Foundation. *Coultas Admission and Dismissal Records and Family File.*

6.   After her unsuccessful interview, Lucretia must have abandoned the idea of a teaching career; by the time of the 1881 Census she had become a Drapers Assistant with Footman & Co. at Waterloo House in Ipswich. Her sister Charlotte Woods Turtill had been christened at Kenton Suffolk on March 21st 1852 and Lucretia was also christened there on October 2nd 1853. They were the daughters of James Woods Turtill and his wife Sarah.

7.   Cockburn, E P. *The Workhouse: Wickham Market, Suffolk.* 1991. Page 11.

8.   *Ibid.* Page 12.

9.   *Ibid.*

10.   Flanders, Judith. *The Victorian House.* 2003. Page 97.

11.   *Minutes of the Wickham Market Work House, Plomesgate Union, Suffolk. 1873–1876.*

12.   *Ibid.*

13.   The George Müller Foundation. *Coultas Admission and Dismissal Records and Family File.*

14.   *Minutes of the Wickham Market Work House, Plomesgate Union, Suffolk. 1873–1876.*

15.   *Ibid.*

16.   The George Müller Foundation. *Coultas Admission and Dismissal Records and Family File.*

Chapter Nine.   New Beginnings

1.   The George Müller Foundation. *Coultas Admission and Dismissal Records and Family File.*

2.   *Ibid.*

3.   Steer, Roger. *Delighted in God, A Biography of George Müller.* 1997. Pages 115–116.

4.   *Ibid.* Pages 136–137.

5.   The George Müller Foundation. *The Bristol Miracle.*

6.   Steer, Roger. *Delighted in God, A Biography of George Müller.* 1997. Page 150.

7.   *Ibid.* Page 151.

8.   *Ibid.* Page 141.

9.   *Ibid.* Page 155.

10.   *Ibid.* Page 152.

11. *Ibid.* Pages 155–156.

12. *Ibid.* Page 156.

13. *Ibid.* Page 148.

14. *Ibid.* Page 184.

Chapter Ten: Out to Service

1. Flanders, Judith. *The Victorian House.* 2003. Page 93.

2. The George Müller Foundation. *The Bristol Miracle.*

3. Steer, Roger. *Delighted in God, A Biography of George Müller.* 1997. Pages 145–147.

4. Flanders, Judith. *The Victorian House.* 2003. Introduction, page xxxix.

5. *Ibid.* Page 96.

6. *Ibid.* Pages 101–102.

7. Glyde Junior, John. *Suffolk in the Nineteenth Century.* 1851.

8. Flanders, Judith. *The Victorian House.* 2003. Page 99.

9. *Ibid.* Page 101.

10. For a full and fascinating account of life for servants in middle-class Victorian households, read Judith Flanders' well-researched book *'The Victorian House'*, particularly Chapter 4, 'The Scullery'.

Chapter Eleven: Marriages and Beyond

1. No doubt it would have been difficult for Susannah to take time off for the wedding as she was in service, but perhaps her employers gave her special permission to accompany her younger sisters to Nottinghamshire for this important occasion.

2. George Coultas, who gave a home on the farm to his nephew Robert Haythorne Coultas when he was orphaned, seems like an interesting

character – everyone's favourite uncle perhaps. In his early twenties it seems he was living back in North Grimston, Yorkshire; possibly he stayed behind with grandparents when his parents moved to Nottinghamshire, or returned when he was older to learn about agriculture before owning his own farm in Lincolnshire. He does not appear to have had children himself. He married Sarah (Denton?), who was nine years younger than him, in 1845 and at the time of the 1881 Census they farmed fifty acres in Langton by Wragby with one fifteen-year-old live-in boy to help, called Thomas Dixon. Staying with George and Sarah and described as a 'visitor' on the night of the Census was thirteen-year-old Louisa Coultas whose birthplace was Liverpool, Lancashire. It seems likely that this Louisa (although not described as 'niece') was the daughter of George's brother William Coultas who lived in Lancashire. George's wife Sarah died two years later and in 1885 at the age of 68 he remarried, this time to Matilda Cook. He died in or near Lincoln in 1898 at the age of 84.

3.   The George Müller Foundation. *The Bristol Miracle.*

4.   Baker-Smith, Veronica. *The Old Rectory, Ubbeston,* in *The Poaching Priors of Blythburgh.* 2002. pages 32–33.

5.   *Kelly's Directory of Suffolk.* 1908.

6.   *Ibid.*

7.   Baker-Smith, Veronica. *The Old Rectory, Ubbeston,* in *The Poaching Priors of Blythburgh.* 2002. pages 32–33.

8.   *Ibid.*

9.   The Rev Watkins would surely have been heartened to know that, despite all his misgivings, his Christian work begun at Fort George (Chisasibi) continues today. The website for St Philips Church in the diocese of Moosonee states that 'Our parish records begin in 1852 with our first recorded marriage performed by Rev Edwin Arthur Watkins who served this parish until the 1860s when we find the Rev John Horden (First bishop of Moosonee) performing the weddings and baptisms for many years. The original Church was built in 1881...that old Church still stands on nearby Fort George Island. The parish is currently home to some 4,000 people (and) is continuing to grow at the rate of more than 100 baptisms per year and between 70 and 90

confirmations a year.' Services are held on Sundays, once in Cree and once in English and a Sunday School meets in the Parish Hall. On Monday there is adult bible study in the Church. The incumbent, appropriately named, is the Rev Jacob Sealhunter.

10.   Woodward, David. *Larn yarself Silly Suffolk*. 1997.

Appendix One: Five Generations of the Coultas Family

Appendix Two: Relatives of the Orphaned Children of James and Eliza Coultas

Acknowledgements

Many people have helped to make this book possible and I am very grateful to all of them. Special thanks go to:

- Wendy Clacker, Administrator of The George Müller Foundation, for very helpful information and for taking time to show me around the most interesting museum at Müller House, 7 Cotham Park, Bristol.
- John S Long in Canada. Without his website I should not have made the exciting discovery that the Rev Edwin Watkins was a missionary to the Cree Indians.
- Gordon Goldsborough (President), Nancy Anderson, Bill Fraser, Judith Hudson Beattie, Myrna Brownlie and other members of the Manitoba Historical Society, Canada, who went out of their way to assist my researches – nothing seemed to be too much trouble.
- The Church Missionary Society for information about the Rev Edwin Watkins.
- The staff at the Suffolk Record Office, Ipswich for their unfailing willingness to help.
- Windsor Ancestry Research (www.windsorancestry.co.uk) who first established that the family of Robert Coultas came from Yorkshire.
- Jeff & Dorothy Bradbury (www.ancestorseeker.com) who carried out further painstaking research in Yorkshire and took photographs of North Grimston Church on a sunny Sunday morning.
- The Church of Jesus Christ of Latter-day Saints for information from their International Genealogical Index. (IGI).
- Jeff Taylor-Jackson for very helpful information about the Allcock family.
- Residents in The Street Parham for permission to include a photograph of their homes.
- Chris Dunford for taking photographs in Bristol.
- Hal Norman of Sudbury, Suffolk, for his skilful editing of the text.
- Richard Franklin and all at arima publishing for their kindness and for making the dream come true.
- Oxford University Press for permission to use the quotation 'The Pathway of a Life Unnoticed' by Horace from The Oxford Dictionary of Quotations, Revised Fourth Edition, 1996, page 348, quotation number 14.
- All other copyright holders who kindly gave their permission for extracts, photographs or illustrations to be used. Every attempt has been made to obtain necessary copyright permission but please accept apologies if there are errors, which will be put right in any future edition.

Printed in the United Kingdom
by Lightning Source UK Ltd.
124682UK00002B/220/A